MW01089003

"The bridge betwe
sive, determined ac
we truly want is tha
trate our power. Nc
Hyatt, and he's eng   ..., easy-to-follow approach to
harness this power in his new book *Free to Focus*."

Tony Robbins, #1 *New York Times* bestselling author,
Unshakeable

"Michael Hyatt is one of America's leading experts in the area
of productivity. He really knows his stuff! That's why I'm so
sure you can absolutely trust what you find in *Free to Focus*.
It will push you to use your time well and to become a better
version of the person you were created to be."

Dave Ramsey, bestselling author and nationally
syndicated radio show host

"I've been where you may be now—buried under a mountain
of daily tasks, watching my biggest goals and most important
projects slip further and further out of reach. Here's the solution. Michael Hyatt has created a productivity system that
really works. *Free to Focus* does not disappoint."

Lewis Howes, *New York Times* bestselling author,
The School of Greatness

"Get off the treadmill! Just running faster won't get you where
you want to be—unless you're chasing the right things. *Free to
Focus* offers a practical, flexible framework for centering your
life around what matters most, and unleashing your best work
every day. Michael Hyatt has helped thousands of people take
back control of their lives, and he'll do the same for you.

Todd Henry, author, *The Accidental Creative*

"Busyness is meaningless. What matters is consistently executing the work that actually matters. This book shows you how."

Cal Newport, *New York Times* bestselling author,
Deep Work and *Digital Minimalism*

"Success, we are often told, requires backbreaking work and
never-ending hours in the office. And then we meet the truly
successful who seem to get more done in less time than anyone else. Michael Hyatt shines the light on the secrets of the
most productive people in his new book, *Free to Focus*. With his

proven methods and research, you'll launch faster, go farther, and perform better than you thought possible."

Skip Prichard, CEO, OCLC, Inc., *Wall Street Journal* bestselling author, *The Book of Mistakes: 9 Secrets to Creating a Successful Future*

"I've known Michael for a long time and this book is one of his best. He hasn't just provided us with a huge chest full of tools, he reminds us why we need them and encourages us to reach for the right one for the job."

Bob Goff, *New York Times* bestselling author, *Love Does* and *Everybody Always*

"At the end of the day, what you create in every area of your life is determined by your ability to focus. What you'll find in *Free to Focus* is a working 'owner's manual' on how to create that focus in every area of your life. Much of what you'll find in this book will be new to you—and maybe even counterintuitive— but it's data-driven from the thousands of clients that Michael has worked with. Read this book and find your focus."

Jeff Walker, #1 *New York Times* bestselling author, *Launch*

"Michael Hyatt is one of the best leaders I know, and I am excited that he's written *Free to Focus*. Michael's use of thorough testing and research, along with his proven track record as a leader of established and start-up companies, translates into a book that is full of insights and practical steps. Leaders rely on smart systems to help them lead in the office as well as at home, and *Free to Focus* provides the kind of system that every smart leader craves."

John C. Maxwell, author, speaker, and leadership expert

"I've had a dozen conversations over the years with friends that have involved the phrase, 'How's Hyatt doing it?' The 'it' in question is 'performing at such a high level and crushing his goals while still enjoying his life and family.' Fortunately, we don't have to wonder anymore because Hyatt has answered that question, and several others, in this fantastic book."

Jon Acuff, *New York Times* bestselling author, *Finish: Give Yourself the Gift of Done*

"You need a system to succeed, and *Free to Focus* can be that system. Michael's no-nonsense, all-helpful advice can help anyone prioritize their life to do more of what's important to them."

Chris Guillebeau, author, *Side Hustle* and *The $100 Startup*

"Overwork is a pervasive form of personal sabotage. Michael Hyatt presents a well-researched but refreshing alternative that allows us to breathe, play, and connect while still accomplishing the very best we have to offer at work. This book will restore the inner peace that makes work—and life—worthwhile."

Dan Miller, *New York Times* bestselling author,
48 Days to the Work You Love

"*Free to Focus* is terrific. Applying Michael Hyatt's insights from this book will help leaders, executives, individual contributors, teachers, coaches, and moms and dads be more productive and purposeful. His framework and related action steps provide a clear path to greater freedom and increased effectiveness."

Tim Tassopoulos, president and COO, Chick-fil-A, Inc.

"Don't work on another project, don't say yes to another opportunity or tackle another task before reading this book. It's that important! Hyatt's *Free to Focus* is my new productivity framework for finding the high-leverage work and maintaining the daily focus I need to see big results on the projects that matter most."

Amy Porterfield, host, *The Online Marketing Made Easy Podcast*

"If you're desperate to tame your to-do list, look no further. Michael Hyatt has a rare genius for cutting complexity and creating simple, practical solutions. *Free to Focus* delivers real results."

Hal Elrod, international bestselling author,
The Miracle Morning

"There are 1,440 minutes in a day, and once they're gone, you never get them back. Michael Hyatt has written a fantastic guide—filled with actionable advice and tools—to maximize your energy, your focus, and results."

Kevin Kruse, *New York Times* bestselling author, *15 Secrets Successful People Know About Time Management*

"Michael Hyatt's practical approach to productivity isn't just another tactical guide filled with good ideas—it's a comprehensive strategy for overhauling your life. It's not just about getting more done, but getting the right things done—and that starts by knowing where you want to go."

Ruth Soukup, *New York Times* bestselling author,
Do It Scared

"Great stories are thought through before they're written. Great lives are the same. Mike gives us a framework to plan our lives in such a way that we won't have to experience regret. This is a great book."

Donald Miller, *New York Times* bestselling author;
founder and CEO, StoryBrand

"Michael Hyatt masterfully blends the best research available with practical steps to help people finally understand what's important—learning to focus and radically improve their productivity. *Free to Focus* is filled with compelling, real-life stories of people who achieved extraordinary results based on the principles found in this book. I'm already using it!"

Ian Morgan Cron, bestselling author, *The Road Back to You*

"Michael Hyatt has written the guide to creating freedom and money without burning ourselves out in the process. At the end of *Free to Focus*, you will be able to work in a space where nothing is urgent, deadlines are met, and the workday truly ends at the office. Hyatt doesn't just teach this material, he lives it."

Brooke Castillo, founder, The Life Coach School

"My experience with leaders causes me to believe that our ability to focus has never been as challenged as it is today. In today's 'respond right now' environment, focus is exactly what will change the game for many of us. For the past two decades, I have observed Michael's immense ability to focus as the CEO of a large organization, an entrepreneur, an author, and a coach. This book is sure to elevate your productivity!"

Daniel Harkavy, CEO and executive coach of Building Champions, coauthor (with Michael Hyatt) of bestselling book, *Living Forward*

"Of all the skills you could master to improve your productivity and results, focus is king, and Michael Hyatt has outlined a masterful plan to achieve focus at the highest level. The steps in *Free to Focus* are clear, the strategies are actionable, and the lessons are timeless. Like me, you may find yourself wanting to reread this powerful book again and again."

Jeff Sanders, speaker and author, *The 5 AM Miracle*

"Everyone has opinions on how to be more productive in our hyper-distracted world, but almost no one has a system backed by sound science. This book is engaging, inspiring, and backed by hard data. In this age where we seem to have more to do but less time than ever, *Free to Focus* is a guiding light for executing our most important goals and freeing up time for what matters most."

Shawn Stevenson, international bestselling author,
Sleep Smarter

"Michael Hyatt has been teaching about personal productivity for years, and it shows with this book. While reading *Free to Focus*, it was almost spooky the number of times my mind would make a straw man argument, and in the very next paragraph, Michael would raise the point of my resistance and resoundingly knock it down. In today's world, being productive is all about making tough choices, and this book gives you the tools you need to do so."

David Sparks, podcast, author, and blogger,
Mac Power Users

"When we're driven, we all wish we had more time. Why? So we could accomplish more, of course! And that's what I love about Michael's book *Free to Focus*. It's not about jamming more into an already full day. This is about proven strategies, backed by tons of research that just happens to fly in the face of conventional wisdom—all of which helps you do more with less. If you've ever felt squeezed for time, wishing you could do more but wondering how to fit it all in, read this book today!"

Stu McLaren, founder, the *Tribe* Course

"If you were told that there was a system that would allow you to get more done and get more time back in your life, I suspect your response would be, 'Yes, please!' Michael Hyatt has done the research, tested the plan, and delivered those results to thousands. Now, in *Free to Focus*, Michael shows us how to move from being busy to being better."

Ken Coleman, podcast host, *The Ken Coleman Show*;
author, *The Proximity Principle*

"In *Free to Focus*, Michael Hyatt drops value bombs on every single page. My biggest aha moment was the power of no. The realization that every time I say yes to something I'm actually saying no to everything else I could be doing is a game changer. With *Free to Focus*, Michael Hyatt is truly *on fire!*"

John Lee Dumas, podcast host, *Entrepreneurs on Fire*

"Michael Hyatt has written a masterpiece on optimizing your productivity and hitting big goals. The book includes a comprehensive system for getting results and a filter for identifying the biggest needle-moving activities in your company. The thing I love most about this book is the system conforms to your life, so it's relevant to anyone in any business. This is undoubtedly Michael's Hyatt's best book yet!"

Josh Axe, founder, DrAxe.com; author, *Eat Dirt*;
CVO, Ancient Nutrition Company

"One of the best personal productivity books I've ever read. *Free to Focus* offers a winning formula for personal and professional achievement."

Mike Vardy, productivity strategist
and founder of TimeCrafting

"I love this book! Michael Hyatt has proven the system where it counts—in the field, with real entrepreneurs, and real corporate leaders. *Free to Focus* isn't just a collection of ad hoc tips. It's a system that's been proven by research, a system that helps you get traction and make real progress on your most important projects. I highly recommend it."

Steven Robbins, creator, Get-it-Done Groups;
podcast host, *Get-It-Done Guy's Quick and Dirty Tips
to Work Less and Do More*

"Whenever I hear of a new productivity topic, I always ask, 'Has Michael Hyatt done research on this yet?' As one of thousands of people who have gone through his *Free to Focus* course, I'm proud to claim Michael as my go-to authority."

Erik Fisher, host, *Beyond the To-Do List* podcast

FREE
TO
FOCUS

FREE
TO
FOCUS

MICHAEL HYATT

EMBASSY BOOKS
www.embassybooks.in

Free to Focus
© 2019 by Michael Hyatt

This edition first published in 2019

Published in India by:
Embassy Book Distributors
120, Great Western Building,
Maharashtra Chamber of Commerce Lane,
Fort, Mumbai - 400 023.
Tel : (91-22) 22819546 / 22818567.
Email : info@embassybooks.in
Website : www.embassybooks.in

Distribution Centres:
Mumbai, Bangalore, Kolkata, Chennai,
Hyderabad, New Delhi, Pune

ISBN: 978-93-88247-66-5

Printed at SAP Print Solutions Pvt. Ltd.

Contents

Stepping into Focus

What will your life have been, in the end, but the sum
total of everything you spent it focusing on?

OLIVER BURKEMAN

think I'm having a heart attack!" Of all ways to end a
relaxing dinner, this is among the worst.

I was a publishing executive in Manhattan on business. A colleague and I were finishing a delicious meal after
a busy day when the chest pain began. I didn't want to
concern my friend or embarrass myself, so I ignored it for a
while, hoping it would pass. It didn't. I smiled and laughed
but heard less and less of what my friend was saying. I was
beginning to panic but tried to keep up appearances. The
pain intensified. The room closed in. Finally, I just blurted
it out.

My friend jumped into action. He paid our bill, hailed
a cab, and rushed me to the nearest hospital. After some

preliminary tests, the doctor reported that all my vitals were fine. I wasn't having a heart attack after all. After a thorough checkup, my primary care physician didn't find any problems either. I was okay! Except I wasn't. I found myself back in the hospital two more times over the next year. Each of these events turned out exactly like the first. Doctors kept telling me my heart was good, but I knew something was wrong.

In desperation, I made an appointment with one of the top cardiologists in Nashville, where I live. He ran me through a battery of tests and called me into his office as soon as the results came in. "Michael, your heart is fine," he said. "In fact, you're in great shape. Your problem is twofold: acid reflux . . . and stress." He said a third of the people he sees for chest pains actually suffer from acid reflux, and most are neck-deep in stress. "Stress is something you need to address," he warned me. "If you don't make this a priority, you could be back in here with a real heart problem."

I was exactly like the overworked, overstressed people he told me about. Work had been insane for as long as I could remember. It never seemed to slow down. At the time I was leading a division in my company, attempting a near-impossible turnaround (more on that later). I already had more priorities than I could count. I was being pulled a hundred different directions. I was the center of every process. I got every phone call, every email, every text. I was on duty 24/7 in a nonstop whirlwind of projects, meetings, and tasks—not to mention emergencies, interruptions, and distractions. My family was weary, my energy and enthusiasm were waning, and now my health was suffering. Something had to give.

Life in the Distraction Economy

My problem back then was doing too much—mostly by myself. Later I realized focusing on *everything* means focusing on *nothing*. It's almost impossible to accomplish anything significant when you're racing through an endless litany of tasks and emergencies. And yet this is how many of us spend our days, weeks, months, years—sometimes, our entire lives.

We should know better by now. We've been doing business in the so-called Information Economy for decades. In 1969 and 1970 Johns Hopkins University and the Brookings Institution sponsored a series of conferences on the impact of information technology. One speaker, Herbert Simon, was a Carnegie Mellon professor of computer science and psychology who later won a Nobel for his work in economics. In his presentation, he warned that the growth of information could become a burden. Why? "Information consumes the attention of its recipients," he explained, and "a wealth of information creates a poverty of attention."[1]

Information is no longer scarce. But attention is. In fact, in a world where information is freely available, focus becomes one of the most valuable commodities in the workplace. But for most of us, work is the hardest place to find it. The truth is we live and labor in the Distraction Economy. As journalist Oliver Burkeman says, "Your attention is being spammed all day long."[2] And stemming the flow of inputs and interruptions can seem impossible.

Consider email. Collectively, we send over two hundred million emails every minute.[3] Professionals start the day hundreds deep with hundreds more on the way.[4] But don't stop there. Toss in the data feeds, phone calls, texts, drop-in visits, instant messages, nonstop meetings, and surprise problems that flood our phones, computers, tablets, and workplaces. Research shows we get interrupted or distracted every three minutes on average.[5] "Even though digital technology has led to significant productivity increases," says Rachel Emma Silverman of the *Wall Street Journal*, "the modern workday seems custom-built to destroy individual focus."[6]

We've all experienced it. Our devices, apps, and tools make us think we're saving time, being hyperproductive. In reality most of us just jam our day with the buzz and grind of low-value activity. We don't invest our time in big and important projects. Instead, we're tyrannized by tiny tasks. One pair of workplace consultants found "about half the work that people do fails to advance [their] organizations' strategies." In other words, half the effort and hours invested produce no positive results for the business. They call it "fake work."[7] We're doing more and gaining less, which leaves us with a huge gap between what we want to achieve and what we actually accomplish.

What It Costs Us

The cost of all this misspent time and talent is staggering. Depending on the studies you consult, the total time lost per day for office workers is three hours or more—as many as six.[8] Let's say you work 250 days a year (365 days, less weekends and two weeks of vacation). That's between 750 and 1,500 hours of lost time every year. The annual hit to the US economy rises as high as $1 trillion.[9] But that's too abstract.

Think instead about the stalled initiatives, postponed projects, and unrealized potential—specifically, *your* stalled initiatives, postponed projects, and unrealized potential. I've consulted with thousands of busy leaders and entrepreneurs over the years, and that's what I hear most from my clients. The dollar value on lost productivity does matter, but it's not what really hurts. It's all the dreams left unexplored, the talents left untried, the goals left unpursued.

Between the projects we want to accomplish and the deluge of other activity—some which is legitimately important and some which only masquerades as such—we're left feeling drained, disoriented, and overwhelmed. About half of us say we don't have enough time to do what we want to do, according to Gallup. For those between the ages of 35 and 54 or people with kids younger than 18, the figure is higher—more like 60 percent.[10] Similarly, six in ten surveyed by the American Psychological Association in 2017 said they're stressed at work, and almost four in ten say it's not the result of one-off projects; it's constant.[11] There are upsides to stress, but not when we can't accomplish what matters most and the strain feels unrelenting.

It seems like the only way to absorb these costs is to let work push back our nights and invade our weekends. A study by the Center for Creative Leadership, for instance, found that professionals with smartphones—and that's pretty much all of us now—engage with their work more than seventy hours a week.[12] According to a study commissioned by the software company Adobe, US workers spend more than six hours every day checking email. To preserve time for the rest of the day's work, 80 percent check their email before going in to the office, and 30 percent do it before they even get out of bed in the morning.[13] According to another study, this one by GFI Software, almost 40 percent of us check email after 11:00 at night, and three quarters of us do it on the weekends.[14] Anecdotally, this seems just as bad, possibly worse, with team chat apps like Slack.

It's like we're working on the wrong side of the Looking Glass. "*Here*, you see, it takes all the running *you* can do, to keep in the same place," the Red Queen tells Alice. "If you want to get somewhere else, you must run at least twice as fast as that!"[15] To manage the pace, some people resort to amphetamines and psychedelics to give them an edge.[16] Even if we grant the supposed benefits of cognitive-enhancing drugs and downplay health and social concerns, what kind of world are we creating where we have to tweak our neurochemistry to stay competitive?

This kind of running carries costs of its own. Not only does it directly contribute to the feeling of unrelenting stress, but long work hours deprive our health, relationships, and personal pursuits of the kind of time they deserve. Hustle into the evening, and your sleep suffers. Leave early for the office, and you skip your morning run. Check email at your kids' soccer game, and you miss the game-winning play. Catch up on a presentation, and you must reschedule that date with your spouse . . . again.

The costs come down to trade-offs. Every day we're constantly making value judgments, deciding what's truly worth our focus. Early in my career, I'm afraid to say, I chose busyness far too often. Now I know these trade-offs make it impossible to give my high-value tasks, health, relationships, and personal pursuits the time and attention—the focus—they deserve. And, as Oliver Burkeman asks, "What will your life have been, in the end, but the sum total of everything you spent it focusing on?"[17]

The pace of work in the Distraction Economy can be relentless. How often do you feel like Alice, running as fast as you can just to stay in place—and twice as fast as that to get ahead?

Counterproductive Productivity

To offset these costs, many of us turn to productivity systems. If we're falling behind like Alice, we figure, maybe we can run faster! So we Google tips and hacks. We troll Amazon and the App Store for ideas and tools to manage our time and boost our efficiency.

That's what I did. After my heart scare, I knew my pace wasn't sustainable. There had to be a better way. I studied every productivity system I could. I tried, tinkered, and tweaked all of them. Little by little it made a difference, and I began sharing my discoveries and applications. That's why I launched my blog fifteen years ago. It was a productivity laboratory for me and my readers. Even though I was then CEO of a major publishing company, I was getting recognized as a productivity expert. Later I founded a leadership development company and now coach hundreds of clients and teach thousands more about productivity every year.

In those early days, I was looking for a way to do more—or at least the same amount a little faster—without killing myself. But I quickly found that keeping pace with the Red Queen wasn't the answer. The breakthrough came when I realized most productivity "solutions" actually make things worse. When I begin working with entrepreneurs, executives, and other leaders, they usually tell me productivity is about doing more and doing it faster. That's because our instincts about productivity come from the age of manufacturing when people performed a defined set of repeatable tasks and could improve the bottom line with marginal gains in execution. But that's not my job. It's not the job of the people I coach. And I bet it's not yours either. Today we have amazing variety in our tasks and we contribute to the bottom line with new and significant projects, not small improvements on existing processes.

And that's the root of the problem. By approaching productivity with the old mindset, we invite the burnout we're trying to avoid and fail to reach our true potential. No one can keep up with the Red Queen. And running faster doesn't help if you're pointed in the wrong direction. It's time to rethink the whole model.

A New Approach

The most productive business leaders I coach recognize productivity is not about getting more things done; it's about getting the right things done. It's about starting each day with clarity and ending with a sense of satisfaction, accomplishment, and energy to spare. It's about achieving more by doing less, and this book shows you how. *Free to Focus* is a total productivity system that follows three simple steps, composed of three actions each. I've arranged the steps to help you gain momentum as you go, so resist the temptation to jump ahead.

Step 1: Stop. I know what you're thinking: "Stop? That can't be the right word. Shouldn't the first step in a productivity system be *Go*?" No. In fact, that's where most productivity systems get it wrong. They jump right to showing you how to work better or faster, but they never stop to ask, *Why? What's the purpose of productivity?* There's a lot at stake with the answer. Unless you first know *why* you're working, you can't properly evaluate *how* you're working. That's why *Free to Focus* suggests to truly start you must stop.

For the first action, you'll *Formulate*. This will help you clarify what you want out of productivity. We'll reframe productivity so it works in the real world, instead of the wrong side of the Looking Glass. Second, you'll *Evaluate*, identifying and filtering your high-leverage activity from low-leverage busy work. You'll also discover a tool that, if used correctly, will completely revolutionize how, when, and where you spend most of your energy. Finally, you'll *Rejuvenate* by discovering how to leverage rest to boost your results.

Step 2: Cut. Once you have a clear view of where you are and what you want, it's time to move to Step 2: Cut. Here you'll discover that what you *don't* do is just as important to

Productivity is not about getting more things done; it's about getting the right things done.

your productivity as what you do. Michelangelo didn't create *David* by adding marble. Ready to break out your chisel? First, you'll *Eliminate.* You'll discover the two most powerful words in productivity and how to use them to banish the time bandits stealing your hours. Second, you'll *Automate*, gaining back time and attention by accomplishing low-leverage tasks in the background without much effort. Finally, you'll *Delegate.* It's a terrifying word for many, but don't worry. I'll reveal an effective method for getting work off your plate and ensuring it gets done to your standards.

Step 3: Act. Having cut out all the nonessentials, it's time for execution. In this section you'll learn how to accomplish your high-leverage tasks in less time and, more importantly, with less stress.

Your first action here is *Consolidate*, which will help you leverage three distinct categories of activity and maximize your focus. Next, you'll *Designate.* By that I mean you'll learn to stage tasks so they fit your schedule and hold back the tyranny of the urgent. Last, you'll *Activate* by eliminating interruptions and distractions and making maximal use of your unique skills and abilities.

Along the way you'll meet some of the clients I've coached who have put these lessons to work in their lives. I'll show you how to do the same thing. Each of the nine actions ends with exercises to help you put these steps into practice right away. Don't skip these activities. They're custom-built to ensure your success. Your days of getting derailed by nonstop interruptions and an out-of-control to-do list are over. Your nights of lying in bed exhausted from a busy day but unsure of what you actually accomplished are done.

It's time to hit the reset button on your life and finally put a system in place that ensures the time and energy to accomplish your most important goals, both in and out of the office.

Can you imagine it? Can you picture when you feel fully in control of where your time is going, when *you* get to decide how to spend your precious energy, and when you hit the pillow at night still energized from a productive, satisfying day? I hope you can, because that time is coming. You really can accomplish more by doing less. Take the first step and discover how.

ASSESS YOUR PRODUCTIVITY

Before we get started, I recommend you stop and complete the Free to Focus Productivity Assessment if you haven't already done so. Go to FreeToFocus.com/assessment. It's quick, easy, and essential to get a baseline of your current productivity. Don't beat yourself up if your score is low. That's why you bought this book, right? You're already aware of some problems, so there's no point trying to hide them now. And, if you score high, don't think you're ready to set this book aside just yet. No matter how well you're doing now, there is always another level of success for those dedicated to pursuing it. Get your personal productivity score at Free ToFocus.com/assessment.

STOP

1

Formulate

Decide What You Want

"Would you tell me, please, which way I ought to go from here?"

"That depends a good deal on where you want to get to."

ALICE AND THE CHESHIRE CAT

Remember the scene from *I Love Lucy* where Lucy and Ethel get hired at a chocolate factory? Their job is to wrap truffles as they come down a conveyor belt. Their manager threatens to fire them if a single chocolate slips by unwrapped. The pair start out okay, but within seconds the sweets are racing by. Lucy and Ethel start shoving them in their mouths and filling their hats with the overflow. When the onslaught finally stops, their manager comes to

Where do we stuff all the extra to-dos, queries, and assignments we encounter on the job? Like Lucy and Ethel, when we successfully manage the overwhelm, our reward is often more work!

inspect their work. She can't see that Lucy and Ethel are hiding all the unwrapped candy, so it appears as if they've kept up and done a good job. Their reward? "Speed it up!" the manager shouts to the person driving the conveyor belt.

Almost everyone I know has felt like Lucy and Ethel at times, including me. Some of us feel like that most of the time. For us, it's not chocolates racing toward us. It's emails, texts, phone calls, reports, presentations, meetings, deadlines—an endless conveyor belt full of new things to do, fix, or think about. We're being as productive as we possibly can, but we can only handle so much.

So we shove the extra tasks into our nights and fill our weekends with projects we can't finish during the workweek. It all piles up on the assembly line in our minds, claiming our mental, emotional, and physical energy. That's what drives us to explore productivity tips and hacks—to find ways to shave a few minutes off each of the million tasks demanding our attention. If we could wrap each chocolate just a split-second faster, maybe, just maybe, we'd be able to keep up. Some of us can make that approach work for us. But it's the wrong approach because it doesn't get at the underlying problem. Either we're too successful in coping with the relentless pace or we're buried by it. Either way, we never stop to ask why we're subjecting ourselves to it in the first place.

So, let's finally stop and ask. What do we want from our productivity? What's the purpose? What are the objectives? True productivity starts with being clear on what we truly want. In this chapter, I'm going to help you formulate your own vision for productivity, one that works for you instead of the manager shouting, "Faster!" This is important, because if we're honest, sometimes that manager is us. On the wrong side of the Looking Glass, sometimes we're not Alice; we're the Red Queen.

To get at the heart of the problem, we'll explore three common productivity objectives. Spoiler alert: The first two are all too common but generally ineffective. The third, however, will be a game changer for you.

Objective 1: Efficiency

Ask a random stranger about the purpose of productivity and there's a good chance you'll hear something about efficiency. This is usually based on the assumption that working faster is inherently better. This easily gets us into trouble, though, because I think people try to work faster just so they can cram even more things into their already-packed day.

Productivity as a concept emerged from the work of efficiency experts such as Frederick Winslow Taylor in the late nineteenth and early twentieth centuries. Applying an engineering background to factory workers, Taylor identified ways to boost efficiency—normally by reducing, even eliminating, workers' autonomy. "The system must come first," he said, and it would have to be "enforced" by management.[1] Taylor instructed managers to dictate workers' methods and routines down to the tiniest details, eliminating any waste or drag. Taylorism, as his approach was known, did produce results. Factories experienced increased efficiency with workers getting more done in less time, but it came at a cost. By limiting employee discretion and freedom, Taylor effectively turned them into manufacturing robots.

Taylor died more than a hundred years ago, but we're still trying to follow the same basic efficiency model: working a lot of hours and doing as many tasks as possible as quickly as we can. The problem is most of us aren't factory workers; we're knowledge workers. We're hired more for our mental output than our physical labor. As such, we often have tremendous discretion over our time and a great deal of autonomy as we go about our daily tasks. While twentieth-century factory workers did the same set of tasks all day every day throughout the week, we are constantly surprised by new challenges, opportunities, and problems. All these things require a tremendous amount of mental energy not only to figure out solutions but sometimes just to keep up.

Taylor's goal was to find ways to work faster. When you apply that to the knowledge economy, however, the work never seems to end. There's always a new idea to consider or problem to solve, and when we do a good job and complete our work, we're rewarded with—you guessed it—more work. We're stuck in the proverbial hamster's wheel, running as hard and fast as we can but never making any real progress on our ever-growing list of projects and tasks. We're too afraid that if we slow down, we'll fall hopelessly behind. If we try to get off the wheel, we may never get back on, so we just keep running. Why do you think most people check their work email on their cell phones all day, all night, and all weekend—even on vacation? It's because they're terrified to let it pile up for a few hours, a day, or—heaven forbid—an entire week.

"Productivity to me looked like just getting more done," one of my coaching clients, Matt, told me. As the founder and CEO of a multimillion-dollar heating and plumbing business, he said he was always concerned with how he could get more accomplished. "The more you get done, then the more time you have to do something else—and just always jumping on whatever comes up. So if I had more margin I could get more done, which would produce more income and more projects. It's always about more."

We'll come back to Matt's story later. For now it's enough to say, the important question is not, *Can I do this job faster, easier, and cheaper?* It's, *Should I be doing this job at all?* Getting clear on that question is more important now than ever, as technology gives us unprecedented access to information, other people, and, of course, our work. We can now work wherever and whenever we want. Our technological marvels haven't made things better. In fact, they've made things worse. The promise of the smartphone was that it would make it easier for us to get our work done, improve efficiency, and give us more time to focus on things that matter. But has your smartphone or tablet magically given you more free time? I bet it's done just the opposite.

Theoretically, we can be more efficient than at any other time in history. As recently as fifteen years ago, most people wouldn't have been able to imagine all we can do today with the supercomputers in our pockets. We can call, email, schedule, manage tasks, videoconference, review spreadsheets, create documents, read reports, message clients, book trips, order supplies, create presentations, and do practically anything else right from our phones. We can close deals between stoplights and check invoices while waiting in line at the grocery store—and you don't even have to wait in line because you can just order those groceries from an app.

I love tech. I'm a certifiable geek! But I understand tech a lot better now than I did early on. New tech solutions may enable us to work faster, but more significantly, that efficiency brings with it the temptation and expectation to work *more*. We take all the time we save with efficiency hacks and use it to squeeze even more tasks into our days. We've figured out a way to speed up our own conveyor belts, and now we're drowning in chocolates with no place left to stuff the overflow.

Objective 2: Success

If efficiency isn't the best goal for our productivity efforts, what about increasing our success?

It seems reasonable to assume improved productivity will lead to greater success, right? Well, sort of. Pursuing the vague notion of success in and of itself can lead us into trouble. The problem is, most of us have never stopped to define what success means. It's like running a race with no finish line or leaving for a trip without knowing where we want to end up. With no clear destination, how will we ever know when we've arrived? This is especially problematic here in America, where we too often buy into the *more* myth. We strive for more products, more deliverables, more clients, more profits. That enables us to acquire more stuff: more houses, more toys, more expensive vacations, more cars. This, in turn, can lead to even more work, more stress, and ultimately, more burnout.

Roy is another of my coaching clients. He's a national account manager for a major lumber company, and this was his struggle. "As measured in our industry, I was pretty productive, but I wasn't meeting my own goals, and I had reached a major plateau," he told me. "I was exhausted, I was worn out, I was stressed out and still not accomplishing my goals. So I tried working harder." Already clocking seventy hours a week—sometimes more—Roy thought the only thing that could deliver success was more hustle.

"I just felt like if I kept pushing through I would get to the other side, and it just wasn't true. I really thought more time and hours would help me accomplish my goals, and they just pushed me further into almost burnout." The emotional toll showed up first in his family but then extended to work itself. His ability to work well with his colleagues suffered. He admitted, "I was drained when I started the day and drained when I ended."

It's a vicious cycle, and it is taking a toll on far more of us than just Roy. According to Gallup, the average American workweek is closer to fifty hours than forty. And one in five works sixty hours or more.[2] You might think it's blue-collar workers who clock the longest shifts, but no. It's professionals and office workers who rack up the most hours.[3] In one study of a thousand professionals, nearly all—94 percent—said they clocked fifty hours or more each week. Nearly half that number worked more than sixty-five. Factor in long commutes, family commitments, and other demands, and even marginally overstuffed schedules cause us to steal time from the margins; the same study found professionals spend about twenty to twenty-five hours each week out of the office monitoring work on their smartphones.[4]

We are living in a period of what German philosopher Josef Pieper called "total work," where labor drives life, not the other way around.[5] And the results are, honestly, depressing. More than half of employees say they're fried, 40 percent work weekends at least once a month, a quarter keep plugging away after hours, and half say they can't even leave their desks for a break.[6] When Kronos Incorporated and Future Workplace checked with more than six hundred human resources leaders, 95 percent said burnout is undermining their employee retention efforts. They identified low pay, long hours, and heavy workloads as the three biggest contributors.[7] Unsurprisingly, a recent Global Benefits Attitudes Survey of workers found stressed employees have significantly higher absentee and lower productivity rates than their happier, healthier peers.[8] Most sobering of all, researchers say workplace stress factors in at least 120,000 deaths per year in the US alone.[9] During the 1970s in Japan the problem was so acute, they coined a word for it: *karoshi*, "death by overwork."[10]

Clearly, if our goal in increasing productivity is to achieve some vague notion of "success," we aren't doing it right. Sick, dead, or dying doesn't sound successful to me. We aren't robots. We need time off, rest, time with family, leisure, play, and exercise. We need big chunks of time when we aren't thinking about work at all, when it's not even on our radar. Sometimes, though, the relentless pursuit of "success" keeps us always on, always engaged, and always available. This is a recipe for failure for both you and your employer. Yes, success is a powerful motivator—but only if you understand what success truly means to you.

Objective 3: Freedom

If productivity isn't fundamentally about improving efficiency and increasing success, then what is the goal? Why should we bother? That brings us to the real objective, and *Free to Focus*'s underlying foundation: *productivity should free you to pursue what's most important to you.* The goal, the true objective of productivity, should be freedom. I define freedom four ways.

1. Freedom to Focus. If you want to master your schedule, increase your efficiency and output, and create more margin in your life for the things you care about, you've got to learn how to focus. I'm talking about the ability to zero in and do the deep work that creates a significant impact, work that moves the needle in a big way. You want your work to solve actual problems in your world, to send you to bed every night knowing exactly what you accomplished and what progress you made toward your goals.

Think back over the last couple of weeks. How much of your time were you free to focus—truly concentrate—on your work? To sit down and attack one task with absolute attention: no distractions, no calls or texts or emails, nobody dropping in to say hi or to ask you a question about something that really didn't matter to you? If you're like most of us, I doubt you've had much time like that at all recently.

Productivity should free you to pursue what's most important to you.

Even when we try to hide by working offsite, whether it's at home or a coffee shop, the always-on accessibility of the smartphone and computer leaves an open door to a million different distractions.

As we've already seen, the average employee faces a distraction every three minutes. Later in the book, we'll explore what impact each of those little interruptions has on our ability to focus. Here's a hint: it's not good. And if you just realized that you are almost never focused on one task for more than three minutes at a time, don't get discouraged. You're not alone. This entire system is designed to bring you the focus you've been missing. Trust me, we'll get there.

2. Freedom to Be Present. How many date nights have you spent thinking about, talking about, or worrying about work? How often do you check your work email or messages when you're out with your family or friends? The statistics we've already seen paint a pretty bleak picture of our ability to unplug from the office and focus on our relationships, health, and personal well-being. Even when we're not technically working, we still drag all our unresolved tasks around.

When we can't get free of our work obligations, we can't be fully present to our family and friends or take the necessary downtime. The *Onion* satirized the problem in a piece headlined "Man on Cusp of Having Fun Suddenly Remembers Every Single One of His Responsibilities." Attending a friend's cookout, the man was "tantalizingly close to kicking back" but then remembered "work emails that still needed to be dealt with, looming deadlines for projects . . . and phone calls that needed to be returned." After "teetering on the brink of actually having fun," he "was now mentally preparing for a presentation."[11] We laugh because it's true.

I'm not interested in efficiency that only gives me more time to work longer hours or success that drives me to work when I should be playing. I'm after *productivity*, not efficiency, which means ensuring significant margin that enables me to be fully present wherever I am. When I'm at work, that means I'm fully present at work. When I'm at dinner with my wife, Gail, that means I'm fully present with her. The important people in my life deserve the very best of me, and I don't want to shortchange them just so I can spend extra time and energy worrying about work.

3. Freedom to Be Spontaneous. This may sound silly to some, but I have always prioritized the freedom to be spontaneous. So many of us have our lives meticulously planned out to the last minute, and we won't tolerate any interruptions or deviations. That doesn't sound like an enjoyable way to go through life. Instead, imagine being able to drop whatever you're doing if your kids or grandkids walked in to say hello. That kind of spontaneity only happens when you create margin in your life, and that is the byproduct of real productivity. When you know you have the most important tasks covered and prevent yourself from taking on more than you can comfortably handle, you'll discover the freedom to be spontaneous.

4. Freedom to Do Nothing. We're always on, and we consider it a virtue. But as we'll see, our always-on culture actually undermines our productivity. It also undermines our joy. When Gail and I visited Tuscany, we discovered *la dolce far* *niente*—the sweetness of doing nothing. It's a national skill in Italy. Americans usually feel guilty doing nothing. Admittedly, I sometimes feel unproductive in the middle of non-task time. But that's the point.

Our brains aren't designed to run nonstop. When we drop things into neutral, ideas flow on their own, memories sort themselves out, and we give ourselves a chance to rest. If you think about it, most of your breakthrough ideas in your business or personal life come when you're relaxed enough to let your mind wander. Creativity depends on times of disengagement, which means doing nothing from time to time is a competitive advantage.

Getting the Right Things Done

The kind of freedom I'm talking about may sound inconceivable to you right now, but I promise, it's possible. The first action on the path to becoming free to focus is to get clear on your objective. We've already seen that the best objective should be to free yourself to focus on what matters most to you. As I've said already, productivity is not about getting *more* things done; it's about getting the right things done. That's what this book is all about—to help you achieve more by doing less.

How do we define *less*? The rest of this book will answer that question, but basically, we're talking about cutting away all the tasks that currently eat up your time that you are not passionate about, that are not important to you, and, frankly, that you're not any good at. Amazing things happen when you start focusing primarily on what you do best and eliminate or delegate the rest. You'll experience greater motivation, better results, more margin, and genuine satisfaction in your work and your life.

Far too often we tailor our lives to our work, meaning we allow our work to sit in the middle of our schedules like a whale in a bathtub. Then we try to squeeze everything else in our lives around it. I think we've got it backward. We should design our lives *first* and then tailor our work to meet our lifestyle objectives. It's not far-fetched. I work with hundreds of entrepreneurs and executives each year who do this and hear from thousands more moving that direction. The result is not only improved work but also greater satisfaction across the board.

For this reason companies, including major corporations, have been experimenting with cutting hours and expanding employee choice. They're seeing the payoff. One Toyota plant in Sweden cut shifts down to six hours. Not only were employees able to complete the same amount of work in six hours that previously required eight, but they were happier, turnover went down, and profits went up.[12]

We've known this for a long time. In 1926, Henry Ford made Ford Motors one of the first companies in the US to switch from a six-day workweek to the five-day, forty-hour model we're so familiar with today. At the time, it seemed crazy to business analysts, but Ford was a visionary. As his son and Ford Motors president Edsel Ford explained to the *New York Times*, "Every man needs more than one day a week for rest and recreation. . . . We believe that in order to live properly every man should have more time to spend with his family."[13]

Of course, these changes boosted Ford Motors' team morale, but many were surprised at the impact to the bottom

We should design our lives first and then tailor our work to meet our lifestyle objectives.

line of the business. Productivity skyrocketed. The factory workers had a renewed appreciation for their company and more energy for their work. In the end, with their hours reduced to forty per week and getting entire weekends off, employees actually produced more by working less, taking Ford Motors to even greater heights.[14]

What's Your Vision?

Why start by stopping to discuss our productivity vision? Because jumping to tips, hacks, and apps won't address the most basic issue. The core problem is within ourselves, and it's something we've struggled with for centuries. Basil the Great, bishop of Caesarea in modern-day Turkey, addressed it in the fourth century. "I have indeed left my life in the city," he said, after moving to a monastery, "but I have not yet been able to leave myself behind." Basil compared it to a person who gets seasick on a big ship and tries to find relief by moving to a dinghy. Doesn't work. Instead, he just brings his seasickness with him. The problem, according to Basil, is this: "We carry our indwelling disorders about with us, and so are nowhere free from the same sort of disturbances."[15]

Most of us view shiny new productivity solutions like the seasick man climbing into the dinghy. *Relief, finally!* But they won't help. We think we can solve our problems by moving to a new app or device, but we're simply dragging our core productivity problems along with us. Doing something different, something better, requires rethinking productivity. If we're gunning for greater efficiency or success as the main goal, we'll fail. Productivity should ultimately give you back more time, not require more of you.

My most productive coaching clients pursue the third objective: freedom. What's more, they have a specific vision for what that looks like in their lives. They start with a picture of what they want their lives to look like before they try to fit their jobs into it. They know where they're headed. Importantly, they don't have any special power you don't. They've got agency, and you do too. You get to choose. So, what's it going to be? The endgame is different for everyone, but I hope you are at least starting to formulate a vision for what fewer, more productive work hours could make possible for you. What will you do with the extra time you're going to free up in your life?

Ask yourself what you want, how many hours you want to work, how many items you want on your task list, how many nights and weekends you want to work. What do you want to focus on? Maybe you want to devote more time to work that drives results. There's nothing wrong with this if that's truly what you want. Or maybe you want to devote more time to other life domains, such as spirituality, intellectual pursuits, family, friends, hobbies, community, or something else entirely. It's completely up to you; no one else can—or should—tell you what matters most to you. Once you figure it out, hold on to that *why* for dear life. It will be the star that guides your ship through this exciting voyage; without it, you'll get lost. That's what productivity gives you: the freedom to choose what you want to focus your time and energy on.

Once you complete the following Productivity Vision exercise, you'll be ready for the next chapter. There, you'll have the chance to evaluate how far you've already come toward achieving your vision and where you need to go from here.

CREATE YOUR PRODUCTIVITY VISION

Formulating a new vision for your life is going to require some serious thinking on your part. You need to be able to picture it in your head and get crystal clear on what you want your life to look like and why it matters to you. To get started, complete the Productivity Vision at FreeToFocus .com/tools. Start by defining what your productivity ideal looks like. Then break it down into a few powerful, memorable words. Finally, clarify the stakes by outlining exactly what you stand to gain if you achieve that vision and what you will lose if you don't.

Remember, this is a vision for what your life could look like. You probably don't have the resources to fully realize your vision today, but don't let that stop you from dreaming. *Free to Focus* is designed to help you start making progress toward your destination, and you'll never make any real progress if you don't know where you're going.

2

Evaluate

Determine Your Course

Everybody ends up somewhere in life. A few people
end up somewhere on purpose.

ANDY STANLEY

Before I started my own company, I had the privilege
of serving as the CEO of Thomas Nelson Publishers.
That was a wonderful opportunity, and it came as the
result of many, many years of proving myself by working in
the trenches. For example, years before I took the reins as
CEO, I was an associate publisher, the second in command
of my division. In July of 2000, my boss suddenly resigned,
and I was asked to take his job. That made me the general
manager of Nelson Books, one of the trade book divisions
of Thomas Nelson.

As an associate publisher, I had a sense that something was off with our division, but I was not prepared for what I discovered when I took over. Our area, apparently, was a disaster. Thomas Nelson had fourteen different divisions at the time, and I discovered the one I led was the least profitable. Dead last. "Least profitable," in fact, is a generous way to put it. The truth is, we had actually *lost* money the previous year. People in other parts of the organization were grumbling about how we were pulling the entire company down. Something had to change fast.

Many leaders facing that moment of crisis would have immediately jumped into action and tried any and everything to bring in some additional revenue and turn things around. I had that temptation, of course, but I didn't go that route. What's the point in filling a leaky bucket without first plugging the holes? Instead, the first thing I did was go on a private retreat. I knew I needed some quiet time to fully evaluate where we were, how we got there, and what we should do next.

I had two goals. First, I wanted to get crystal clear on where we were, no matter how grim it was. Second, I wanted to come up with a compelling vision for what I wanted to achieve instead. I was confident that once the start and end points were clear, my team and I would be able to chart a course for getting from where we were to where we wanted to be. And believe it or not, that's exactly what happened.

I thought it would take three years to accomplish my initial vision. Instead, we pulled off a complete turnaround in just eighteen months. Along the way, we exceeded in almost every aspect of our vision, and our once-struggling Nelson Books division became the fastest-growing, most profitable division of Thomas Nelson over the next six years. We went

from dead last to leading the pack, and it didn't happen because we had a great business strategy; it happened because
we had a clear vision of where we wanted to go, and we were
honest about where we were starting from.

Now it's your turn.

The Intersection of Passion and Proficiency

In chapter 1, you began to chart where you want to go. If you
completed the Productivity Vision exercise, you have already
developed a compelling vision for yourself. (If you haven't
completed that activity yet, I recommend stopping now and
finishing it. The chapters and exercises build on each other,
so you can't afford to skip one.)

Now that you know where you want to go, you need to
figure out where you are right now. For that, you're going
to need a special kind of compass—the Freedom Compass.
This tool, which we'll use throughout the rest of the book,
will serve as your productivity guide. It will always be there
to prevent you from heading off in the wrong direction. It
will also help you evaluate tasks, activities, and opportunities
based on two key criteria: passion and proficiency. Getting
a handle on these two things will revolutionize your entire
view of productivity. It's not enough to be either passionate
or proficient at a task you're called upon to do regularly. You
need to be both or your energy and performance will suffer.

By passion, I'm talking about work you love, work that
energizes you. Has there ever been a time in your life when
you were working on something and thought, *I can't believe
they're paying me to do this*? If so, you know what passion
feels like. You're capable of doing many things, but you're

the most motivated and satisfied when you're doing things you love. If you don't love your job, it's hard to stick with it.

Proficiency is something else entirely. Proficiency doesn't refer to how much you enjoy doing something; it describes how well you actually do it. The truth is, there may be something you're extremely passionate about, but if you aren't especially skilled at it, no one will ever pay you to do it. For example, I live in Nashville, Tennessee—Music City, USA. We're crawling with musicians. But most aren't in the music industry; they're waiting tables. I'm sure they're passionate about music, or they wouldn't even bother. I'm sure most of them are fairly skilled too.

> By passion, I'm talking about work you love, work that energizes you.

In any other city in the country, they may be local celebrities. But here in Nashville, it's a totally different game. You can't just be a *good* musician and make it here; you have to be *great* to get attention.

Many people confuse proficiency with aptitude, but they're not the same. Aptitude is an ability or knack for doing something. Proficiency is something more. Proficiency means you're not only skilled at something, you're also generating results that other people can measure and reward. For executives and entrepreneurs, that mostly comes down to revenues, profits, and other financial metrics. For musicians, it could be downloads, sales, crowds, or awards. Aptitude signals skill alone, while proficiency signals skill *plus* contribution. It's what you offer the world that the world rewards. No matter how talented you are, if you're not making a contribution in a certain area, you're not truly proficient.

Aptitude signals skill alone, while proficiency signals skill plus contribution.

Four Zones of Productivity

Now that we're clear on terms, let's look at the mechanics of the Freedom Compass. Start by picturing a grid with Proficiency running across the x axis and Passion running up the y axis. These two criteria will help you identify and understand four different zones that you normally operate in. Before we're done, you'll have a much better understanding of why certain tasks make the day fly by and why others bring it to a screeching halt. We'll review the four zones in reverse order so you can see the progression, and we'll start with the zone we all hate.

Zone 4: The Drudgery Zone. The Drudgery Zone is made up of tasks for which you have no passion and no proficiency. Basically, these are the things you hate doing and aren't any good at anyway. This is the worst kind of work for you to do. It's a grind.

Things like expense reports, handling email, and booking travel fall into my personal Drudgery Zone. I have zero passion and zero proficiency at these things, so making myself do them is a chore. These tasks take longer than they should, and the end result is a lot of wasted time. Why do I say wasted? It's because my time and energy would be much better utilized—and therefore more productive—if I focused on other things, things at which I could make a real contribution. I'm never going to be good at booking travel, and I never want to become good at booking travel. So why should I force myself to do it?

Keep in mind, though, that just because something falls into your Drudgery Zone doesn't mean it falls into everyone's Drudgery Zone. These aren't bad tasks per se; they're

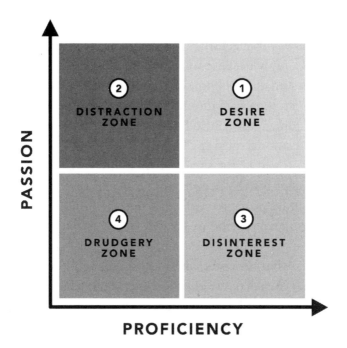

Passion and proficiency provide a helpful grid for evaluating our tasks. When passion and proficiency for particular tasks run high, that's your most desirable work. When they're both low, our tasks feel like drudgery.

just things you personally have no passion or proficiency for. Believe it or not, there are a lot of people in the world who love the things you hate, and vice versa. Without that division of labor, our complex economy wouldn't work.

Zone 3: The Disinterest Zone. The Disinterest Zone is made up of things that you're proficient at, but you aren't that passionate about. Sure, you can do these tasks—maybe better than anyone else in your office—but they drain your energy. Why? It's because you have no passion. Frankly, you just don't care about them, so you get bored doing them.

Most of us are naturally inclined to avoid Drudgery Zone tasks, but we often get stuck in a rut doing Disinterest Zone activities simply because we're good at them.

This is something I know all too well. I mentioned before that I have a long background in publishing. I got into the business long ago because I have always loved books. The great motivational speaker Charlie "Tremendous" Jones used to say, "You will be the same person in five years as you are today except for the people you meet and the books you read." I could not agree with this statement more. In fact, every significant period of growth in my life has been the direct result of either a person I met or a book I read. That passion is what drove me into publishing, and I developed proficiency in each of my positions as I climbed the corporate ladder. The higher I went, though, the less involved I became in the work of making books.

Every promotion led me a little further away from books and a little closer to administration. By the time I became CEO, my job was primarily about finance. I do have an aptitude for finance, and I eventually developed proficiency for it. However, my passion didn't last beyond the initial phase of learning and mastery. Bottom line: it bored me to death. The problem was, that's what I was getting paid to do. Confronting this was one of the key realizations that led me to leave my position and refocus my energy on my first love, creating content. I've heard similar stories from so many people. If we're not careful, we can get stuck in the Disinterest Zone for years, maybe decades, simply because it's what pays the bills.

Zone 2: The Distraction Zone. In this zone, life starts to get a lot more tolerable. The Distraction Zone is made up of things that you are passionate about but sadly have little proficiency for. This means these activities aren't draining your energy and you enjoy doing them, but if you aren't careful, they can be massive time-wasters. The problem is that you aren't proficient at them, which prevents you from making a significant contribution in these areas.

Here's the problem with the Distraction Zone: your passion can mask your lack of proficiency—but only to yourself. Our proficiency is best seen by other people. That means we may be the last to know that we're wasting an enormous amount of time doing subpar work on something we enjoy.

It's not just fair-to-middling musicians in Nashville. It's the finance exec who can't stop interfering with marketing. Or the salesperson who meddles in graphic design. Or the manager who finds it easier to do the team's work than lead the team. Unless these efforts are validated by others (e.g., colleagues, customers, clients, superiors, an audience, the market) as truly—uniquely—valuable, then they're Distraction Zone activities. When we're identifying tasks that fall into our Distraction Zone, we have to be ruthless with ourselves, knowing that we're calling out things we love but probably shouldn't be doing.

Zone 1: The Desire Zone. The Desire Zone is the point where your passion and proficiency intersect, where you can unleash your unique gifts and abilities to make your most significant contribution to your business, family, community . . . and maybe the world. If your destination is freedom, this is where you'll experience it. The rest of the book will be focused on getting you into the Desire Zone and helping you stay there as much as possible throughout the week.

Working in your Desire Zone has a profound effect on personal productivity—and more. It's the best way I know to win at work and succeed at life in general, because you'll do more high-leverage work in less time, which frees up margin for the other domains in life: family, friends, and so on. This is what started making the difference for my client Roy, who we met in the last chapter. "Focusing on my Desire Zone and ditching everything else was big for me," he told me. "Realizing that it's okay to delegate everything—and I do mean everything—that's not in my Desire Zone has been one of the most freeing things I can imagine."

By delegating work outside his Desire Zone, Roy cut his hours from seventy a week to forty on his primary job. I say *primary* because he works another ten hours a week in two passion projects he started with his family. Before he had committed to working at both peak passion and peak proficiency, he didn't have margin for extras like that. His margin was gobbled up with low-leverage tasks that killed his energy and undermined his effectiveness.

Another client, Rene, has a similar story. Rene's company buys and sells private jets. Before she discovered the four zones, she described her life "on a hamster wheel . . . I worked all the time." Understanding this link between passion and proficiency was key to escaping the rat race. "It gave me permission to concentrate on items in my Desire Zone, and really it enabled me to say, 'I don't have to be busy all the time. I can have time just to do deep thinking and deep work on what matters most.'" The impact for Rene was immediate. She cut her weekly hours from sixty to thirty, and she said she reclaimed even more than that. By ordering her tasks, she said, "I'm not distracted by the things that don't matter. So really, I've reclaimed my whole life."

Mariel runs an accounting business and, like many of us, found work pushing into every corner of her life. When we first started working together, she regularly worked sixty to seventy hours a week and never left work at home on vacations. "I had grown up in a family business," she explained. "Working extra hours and working all the time was something I was accustomed to, and I loved work." But she found some work was higher leverage and some lower. "The thing that made the biggest impact on me," she said, "was working through my zones—figuring out what's disinterest, what's drudgery, and where my desire actually was." Once she had a clear sense of that, she was able to eliminate, automate, and delegate tasks outside her Desire Zone (more on that follows in Step 2).

Mariel not only cut thirty hours off her workweek, she also grew her business while working less. And the same is true for Roy and Rene. In fact, it's true for everybody I know who works at the intersection of peak passion and peak proficiency.

Zone X: The Development Zone. There is a fifth zone with no fixed place on the grid. I call it the Development Zone, and it's how to gauge work outside your Desire Zone but potentially moving toward it. Maybe you're high-proficiency/low-passion, but you're developing passion. Or you're high-passion/low-proficiency, but you're building proficiency. This progression is important to keep in mind, because our experience affects both passion and proficiency.

We don't come with default or fixed settings, being either naturally passionate or proficient. Rather, we all begin with curiosity, interest, and possibly some raw talent. Time and practice play a part in where a task falls, and that task can move based on how we evolve in relation to it. In other words, passion and proficiency are the result of personal or professional development.

Several tasks in my Desire Zone today migrated there from the Development Zone. That's true for many. When my daughter Megan Hyatt Miller first started working for me, she had zero passion for financial analysis. She excelled at branding and marketing, but spreadsheets and projections were a grind. She had neither passion nor proficiency. She was, however, willing to learn and possessed some aptitude. With time and training she developed genuine proficiency. And that wasn't all. As Megan developed proficiency, her passion also grew. Research by Florida State University psychologist Anders Ericsson and others shows that practice and eventual mastery can influence the joy we feel in a task. I say *can* because it's not a given; as a publishing CEO, I could hold my own in a room full of bankers, but I rarely enjoyed it. For some, however, practice doesn't just make perfect; it also makes pleasurable.[1] And that's when we notice a task has migrated from one zone to another.

Mindset is another aspect of tasks shifting into our Desire Zone. Megan is visionary and oriented toward the future. In StrengthsFinder language, Futuristic is her number one strength.[2] Part of what drove Megan's growing interest in the numbers was how they played into company goals and strategy. "The financials are how we execute on our vision," she told me. "It's the practical application." Today, financial modeling, cashflow projections, and high-level budgeting are all Desire Zone activities for Megan, who now serves as chief operating officer of MH&Co.

We sometimes know a certain task is not in our wheel-house. Other times we just need more experience with it. If we have a hunch we could develop passion and proficiency with a task, we should stay open-minded about it.

Finding Your True North

Now that you understand the four zones of productivity, let's look at the Freedom Compass itself. You'll see the compass is simply the passion-and-proficiency grid rotated so the Desire Zone occupies the top position. What's one of the most important skills for navigation? Finding true north. Zone 1, the

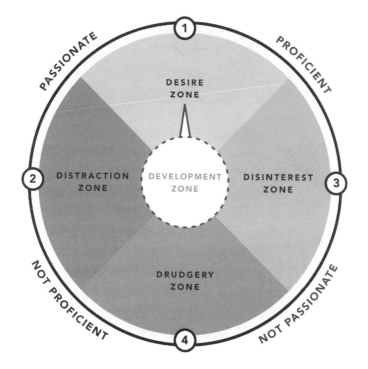

Rotating the passion and proficiency grid creates your Freedom Compass. The more you can steer your efforts north, toward your most desirable work, the more productive you'll be. The adjoining examples show you how the Freedom Compass gives direction to your work.

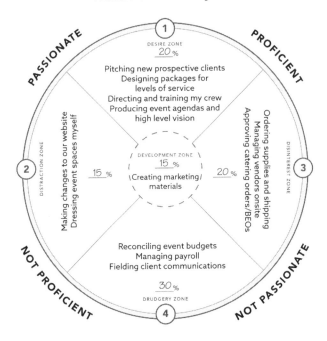

Aleshia
Founder of an Event Management

PASSIONATE · PROFICIENT

1 — DESIRE ZONE — 20%
Pitching new prospective clients
Designing packages for levels of service
Directing and training my crew
Producing event agendas and high level vision

DEVELOPMENT ZONE — 15%
Creating marketing materials

2 — DISTRACTION ZONE — 15%
Making changes to our website
Dressing event spaces myself

3 — DISINTEREST ZONE — 20%
Ordering supplies and shipping
Managing vendors onsite
Approving catering orders/BEOs

4 — DRUDGERY ZONE — 30%
Reconciling event budgets
Managing payroll
Fielding client communications

NOT PROFICIENT · NOT PASSIONATE

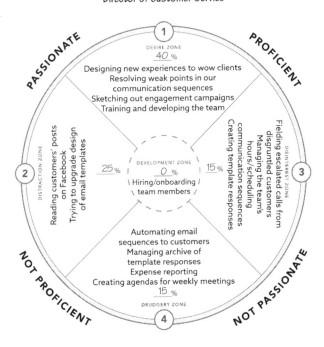

Kevin
Director of Customer Service

PASSIONATE · PROFICIENT

1 — DESIRE ZONE — 40%
Designing new experiences to wow clients
Resolving weak points in our communication sequences
Sketching out engagement campaigns
Training and developing the team

DEVELOPMENT ZONE — 0%
Hiring/onboarding team members

2 — DISTRACTION ZONE — 25%
Reading customers' posts on Facebook
Trying to upgrade design of email templates

3 — DISINTEREST ZONE — 15%
Fielding escalated calls from disgruntled customers
Managing the team's hours/scheduling
communication sequences
Creating template responses

4 — DRUDGERY ZONE — 15%
Automating email sequences to customers
Managing archive of template responses
Expense reporting
Creating agendas for weekly meetings

NOT PROFICIENT · NOT PASSIONATE

Desire Zone, is true north for your productivity. That's the direction you want to head. Just like a navigational compass can save your life if you're lost in the wilderness, the Freedom Compass can guide you through the jungle of meaningless, unproductive work.

The promise of this book is to help you achieve more by doing less, and here's how we're going to do it. This is the secret to productivity that many either take for granted or miss completely. *True productivity is about doing more of what is in your Desire Zone and less of everything else.* Underline that statement. Write it on a Post-it Note and stick it to your computer monitor. Post it in your car. Recite it ten times a day if you need to, but do not miss this point: true productivity is about doing more of what is in your Desire Zone and less of everything else. Focusing your time and energy on your Desire Zone is going to drive results and create freedom. This is the key to achieving more by doing less.

> True productivity is about doing more of what is in your Desire Zone and less of everything else.

The more time you spend in your Desire Zone, the more good you do not only for yourself but also the world around you. I know that's a bold statement, so let me explain. All of us possess unique gifts—a specific package of native talent, acquired skills, drive, and wisdom particular to us as individuals—and we are never more effective, never more powerful, never more influential than when we are exercising those gifts. You can't be me, and I can't be you. However, we can all be the best version of ourselves. I believe that happens when we live and work in our Desire Zone.

One more word on this before we move on: while the *Free to Focus* system can get you into the Desire Zone quickly, it won't happen overnight. Today, I spend about 90 percent of my time on Desire Zone activities, and I want you to join me there as quickly as possible. Stephen, an online sales wizard and coaching client, told me he's now working 80 to 90 percent in his Desire Zone. But he didn't start there. When he first took my *Free to Focus* online course, he realized, "I'm doing all of these things in my Drudgery Zone. . . . I was trying to do everything," including "trying to fix printers, and it was just painful!" If you're responsible for major results, can you afford to mess with the office equipment? When Stephen figured out how much effort he was wasting, he began using the Freedom Compass to point him to his most high-leverage tasks. He not only reclaimed margin—which his young family appreciates—but his business doubled. "It's made a huge impact on the bottom line and given me a lot more joy," he said.

Now that you know about the Freedom Compass, keep your eyes on true north. Do your best to move in the direction right for you using the tools in this book. Be patient along the way. A compass is a guide, not a bull's-eye. It's a pointer, not the point. Maybe there's something you love to do and have aptitude for, but you need to develop proficiency. Or maybe you're perfectly capable and want to find something that stokes your fire. That's fine. Use the Development Zone as a way station where you can put things that you're unsure about but suspect might be important to your business someday, especially if they can improve the results you know you're supposed to produce.

But here's a question: If productivity simply comes down to doing more things in your Desire Zone and less of everything else, why aren't most of us doing that already? Why does this so often seem like an impossible goal?

Limiting Beliefs, Liberating Truths

The biggest obstacle in our efforts to become productive may very well be our mindset. We don't intend for this to happen, but our lives become driven by a collection of beliefs we have about ourselves and our situation. These are *limiting* beliefs, because they limit our potential and establish false, constricting boundaries that prevent us from accomplishing bigger and better things. We could fill a whole book with limiting beliefs, but let's zero in on the seven that most impact our efforts to become more productive.

1. "I just don't have enough time." The limiting belief I hear more than anything else is "I just don't have enough time." Said another way, it's "I'm too busy." I've heard this from every type of person in every walk of life, from CEOs to business professionals, construction workers, stay-at-home moms, and college students. It's a universal truth: we all feel too busy. If you're struggling with this limiting belief, replace it with this liberating truth: *I have all the time I need to accomplish what matters most.* Take a fresh look at the great accomplishments taking place around you and the individuals leading major change in the world. Remind yourself that you have the same 168 hours a week that they do, and you too can accomplish great things in the time you have.

2. "I'm just not that disciplined." People who view productivity in terms of a massive, complicated system full of tagging, filing, tweaking, and listing a million different tasks usually face the limiting belief "I'm just not that disciplined." If that describes you, replace it with this liberating truth: *Working in my Desire Zone doesn't require much discipline.* We usually don't complain about not having enough discipline when it comes to spending time on things we enjoy. We reserve the word discipline for those things we don't want to do. It's a matter of focus. If you design your life so that you spend most of your time working on things you are passionate about and proficient at, the discipline to do those things comes easily.

3. "I'm not really in control of my time." Not everyone is a CEO, self-employed, or even in management. Most of your day may be dictated by your boss or even your family's schedules. However, we too often use these demands as an excuse to throw up our hands and say, "I'm not in control of my time, so it won't work." If you fall victim to this limiting belief, replace it with this liberating truth: *I have the ability to make better use of the time I do control.* You are not a passive object floating through life, completely at the mercy of outside forces. You have a say in how you live your own life. Pockets of time may be under someone else's control, but you still have control over the rest. Make it count.

4. "Highly productive people are just born that way." Sometimes we let ourselves off the hook by saying something like, "Highly productive people are just born that way. I wasn't." This one is just flat-out false. The people you admire most in the world, the people who are achieving great things, were not born with superhuman abilities. They simply found a way to develop their own potential—and you can too. If you fall victim to this limiting belief, replace it with this liberating truth: *Productivity is a skill I can develop*. This book will show you how to do just that.

5. "I tried before, and it didn't work." I wish I had a nickel for every time someone excused their lack of productivity by saying, "I tried that before, and it didn't work." That is definitely not the mantra of high-achievers. In fact, high-achievers never give up simply because one solution failed. Instead, they keep looking for what will work, and they don't stop until they find it. If you've been discouraged by the things that have failed so far, replace that limiting belief with this liberating truth: *I can get better results by trying a different approach*. That's why I created the *Free to Focus* system in the first place—none of the other productivity systems I tried ever worked for me. This one does.

6. "My circumstances won't allow it right now, but they're only temporary." Of all the limiting beliefs we're discussing, the deadliest may be "My circumstances won't allow it right now, but they're just temporary. I'll be more productive later." This belief, even though it seems reasonable and hopeful for the future, can wreck any chance you have of ever becoming more productive. What is temporary will eventually become permanent unless you change something now. Maybe you're facing a busy quarter at work, a heavy season of your children's extracurricular activities, or an unusual uptick in your social or community commitments. Whatever it is, heed this warning: *It is not temporary*. These busy seasons keep redrawing the boundary lines around our time, and things will never go "back to normal." It's up to you to define what you want normal to look like; if you do not take control of your time, someone else will. We cannot keep postponing our progress. Instead, we need to embrace this liberating truth: *I don't have to wait until my circumstances change to get started and make progress.* If you wait for the perfect time to become more productive and pursue the freedom you crave, you'll be waiting forever. You can start making positive changes right now, regardless of your circumstances.

7. "I'm not good with technology." You may struggle with the limiting belief that says, "I'm not good with technology or complicated systems." We're all looking for a simple, elegant solution—and that's honestly hard to find in the world of productivity. If you find yourself scratching your head at the multitude of different, complicated productivity apps, tools, and systems out there, embrace this liberating truth: *True productivity doesn't require complex technology or systems. It's more about aligning my daily activities with my priorities, and I can do that.* Anyone can do that, in fact, but it begins with believing you can.

These are the seven limiting beliefs I've heard most often over the years, but the list is by no means exhaustive. In fact, many new limiting beliefs may have popped into your head as you read through these. Our mindset is something we often overlook on our way to becoming more productive, but that oversight can undermine even our best efforts if we aren't careful. If you don't address the voices in your head, you'll never get a clear picture of where you are now, which means you'll never be able to navigate to where you want to go.[3]

Limiting Beliefs	Liberating Truths
I just don't have enough time.	I have all the time I need to accomplish what matters most.
I'm just not that disciplined.	Working in my Desire Zone doesn't require much discipline.
I'm not really in control of my time.	I have the ability to make better use of the time I do control.
Highly productive people are just born that way.	Productivity is a skill I can develop.
I tried before, and it didn't work.	I can get better results by trying a different approach.
My circumstances won't allow it right now, but they're only temporary.	I don't have to wait until my circumstances change to get started and make progress.
I'm not good with technology.	True productivity doesn't require complex technology or systems. It's more about aligning my daily activities with my priorities, and I can do that.

The goal of this chapter has been to guide you in evaluating your current situation. For some, this can be the hardest part of the *Free to Focus* process. But it's central to everything that follows. Once you finish the following exercise, we have one final action to complete Step 1. It's time to talk about rejuvenation.

REDIRECT YOUR TASKS

Evaluating your current position is a vital step toward your productivity goals, but it's one many people skip. If you don't take a hard, honest look at where you are and how you got there, you'll never be able to move ahead as far and as fast as you want to.

Use the Task Filter and Freedom Compass worksheet at FreeToFocus.com/tools. List your regular tasks and activities on the Task Filter. Once you've got your list, evaluate each item by passion and proficiency. Then use that insight to determine to which zone each task belongs. (Ignore the Eliminate, Automate, and Delegate columns for now; we'll come back to those later.)

Once you've categorized your tasks, take an extra minute to transfer them to your Freedom Compass, listing each task in its appropriate zone. Place any Development Zone activities in the center. Post your completed Freedom Compass where you'll see it often and use it as a reminder to focus on Desire Zone activities as much as possible.

3

Rejuvenate

Reenergize Your Mind and Body

Almost everything will work again if you unplug it for
a few minutes, including you.

ANNE LAMOTT

University of Pennsylvania professor Alexandra Michel, a former Goldman-Sachs employee, conducted
a twelve-year study of investment bankers who regularly worked between 100 and 120 hours a week. There are
only 168 hours in a week. As we saw in chapter 1, entrepreneurs, executives, and other professionals already steal time
from the margins with fifty-plus-hour workweeks. To work
120 hours means shortchanging *everything* else in life: sleep,
relationships, exercise, recreation, spiritual and community
activities, and more. To offset the loss, the bankers' employer

offered them round-the-clock administrative aid, meal and laundry services, and other domestic assistance.

Given their singular focus, the bankers were highly productive at the start. They came in with energy and vigor, took advantage of the extra services their employer provided, and worked hard and long, making huge strides. But it didn't last. It couldn't last.

"Starting in year four, bankers started to experience sometimes debilitating physical and psychological breakdowns," Michel reported. "They suffered from chronic exhaustion, insomnia, back and body pain, autoimmune diseases, heart arrhythmias, addictions, and compulsions, such as eating disorders, causing them to exhibit diminished judgment and ethical sensitivity." As their performance plummeted, Michel said, "They simply compensated for their diminishing output by working longer, which caught them in a cycle of escalating work hours and chronic physical and emotional distress."[1]

We're chasing our tails when we try this approach. Jack Nevison, founder of New Leaf Project Management, crunched the numbers from several different studies on long work hours. He found there's a ceiling. Push past fifty hours of work in a week and there's no productivity gain for the extra time. In fact, it goes backwards. One of the studies he examined found that fifty hours on the job only produced about thirty-seven hours of useful work. At fifty-five hours, it dropped to almost thirty. The more you work beyond a fifty-hour threshold, according to this study, the less productive you become. Nevison calls this the Rule of Fifty.[2]

That means, based on the number of hours most of us work, we're on the edge of working backwards if we're not doing so already. UC Berkeley management professor

Morten T. Hansen compares overlong hours to squeezing an orange. "At first," he says, "you get a lot of liquid. But as you continue to squeeze and your knuckles turn white, you extract a drop or two. Eventually, you reach the point where you're squeezing as hard as you can, but producing no juice."[3] In one revealing study, managers found no measurable difference between the performance of workers who clocked 80 hours a week and those who simply faked it; the additional hours resulted in no real productivity gains.[4] By working to the point of exhaustion, we are achieving less by doing more—the opposite of what we want. To achieve more by doing less, though, we must let go of some of our closely held misconceptions about time and energy.

The bankers fell prey to a common productivity myth: that energy is fixed, but time can flex. They believed they could get a consistent return on their effort while expanding their hours—that they'd be just as smart, strong, and engaged at 100 hours as they were at 50. Here's Elon Musk,

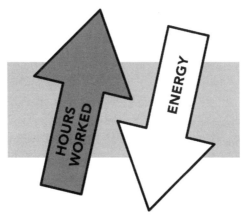

Time is fixed, but energy can flex. That means there's an inverse relationship between hours worked and the productive expense of your energy. The more hours you work, the less productive you'll be.

founder and CEO of Tesla and SpaceX, in a classic statement of the fallacy: "If other people are putting in 40-hour workweeks and you're putting in 100-hour workweeks, then even if you're doing the same thing . . . you will achieve in four months what it takes them a year to achieve."[5] But the bankers and Musk have it exactly backwards. One hundred hours of work is qualitatively, not merely quantitatively, different than fifty. Time is fixed, but energy can flex. Every day contains the same number of hours, while your energy swings up and down depending on multiple variables, including rest, nutrition, and emotional health.

> Time is fixed, but energy can flex.

Most of us know this intuitively. When we're fresh in the morning, we can accomplish twice as much as we do after lunch. That's energy flexing. The good news is that you can make your energy flex in your favor so you get the most juice for the least squeeze. That's what this action, Rejuvenate, is all about. Personal energy is a renewable resource, replenished by seven basic practices. We must:

1. Sleep
2. Eat
3. Move
4. Connect
5. Play
6. Reflect
7. Unplug

Let's start by looking at the first.

Practice 1: Sleep

Eulogizing one of his top executives, former Disney CEO Michael Eisner said, "Sleep was one of [his] enemies. [He] thought it kept him from performing flat out 100 percent of the time. There was always one more meeting he wanted to have. Sleep, he thought, kept him from getting things done."[6] We all buy into that myth at times, but it's nothing to celebrate. We convince ourselves we can squeeze one more meeting or task into the day if we get up earlier or go down later. It's pervasive.

On average Americans get just under seven hours of sleep each night.[7] And that number, already below the recommended eight, is probably overstated because people usually report the time they spend in bed, not the hours they actually sleep. We get about 20 percent *less* sleep than we think, according to researchers.[8] And that's the average! In the business world, we boast about getting even less.

Leaders at PepsiCo, Southwest, Fiat Chrysler, Twitter, and Yahoo! have all claimed to thrive on half the recommended amount of sleep.[9] The bragging rights go up as the time in bed goes down, creating a self-imposed expectation among entrepreneurs and leaders at every level. If you want to be among the best and brightest, you're supposed to be superhuman. But we're not superhuman. Two-thirds of leaders in one survey expressed dissatisfaction with the amount of sleep they get, and more than half lamented low-quality sleep.[10] It comes at a high cost.

We treat the pillow like the enemy of productivity, but skipping sleep ultimately hurts our work. *The Lancet*, for instance, studied surgeons who stayed awake twenty-four hours. The doctors made more mistakes, and routine tasks took them 14 percent longer. The impairment was on par with being intoxicated.[11] And it doesn't take one all-nighter for those kinds of results. In another study, people getting just six hours a night for two straight weeks functioned as if they were legally drunk.[12] Rather than boosting productivity, we're ensuring our own failure when we rob our rest.

Nightly rejuvenation is the foundation of productivity. Sufficient sleep keeps us mentally sharp and improves our ability to remember, learn, and grow. It refreshes our emotional state, reduces stress, and recharges our bodies. Meanwhile, going without sleep makes it harder to stay focused, solve problems, make good decisions, or even play nice with others.[13] As neuroscientist Penelope A. Lewis explains, "Sleep-deprived people come up with fewer original ideas and also tend to stick with old strategies that may not continue to be effective."[14]

That's precisely why effective leaders and entrepreneurs stress getting adequate sleep. Consider Amazon CEO Jeff Bezos. "Eight hours of sleep makes a big difference for me," he told Thrive Global. "That's the needed amount to feel energized and excited."[15] Aetna chairman and CEO Mark Bertolini actually offers cash incentives for employees to prioritize their sleep. "You can't be prepared if you're half-asleep," he explained in an interview. "Being [fully] present in the workplace and making better decisions has a lot to do with our business fundamentals."[16]

Rejuvenating rest comes down to two things: quantity and quality. Adults—regardless of what's on their calendars or who is demanding their time and attention—require seven to ten hours of sleep a night to perform at their peak. You need to give yourself permission to sleep as much as you find necessary to be at your best. Admittedly, that can be difficult. If your schedule is packed, you might need to sacrifice time on Facebook or Netflix ("We're competing with sleep," Netflix CEO Reed Hastings has admitted).[17] If you have young children, you and your partner may need to sleep in shifts or even hire an overnight babysitter occasionally to ensure undisturbed rest. You might even consider going to bed at the same time your kids do for a few nights to get some extra *zzz*'s.

You can also increase your quantity of sleep by adding a short nap to your daily schedule. Don't laugh; naps are my secret productivity weapon. I take one every day after lunch, and it keeps me fresh and alert all afternoon. Just don't nap longer than twenty or thirty minutes, or you may have a hard time waking up and you'll feel groggy, not reinvigorated. There's a long list of leaders, artists, scientists, and others who have improved their performance by strategic napping. To name just a few: Winston Churchill, Douglas MacArthur, John F. Kennedy, J. R. R. Tolkien, and Thomas Edison.[18] Don't be surprised if it takes a while to get the hang of it. "Like skydiving, napping takes practice," says essayist Barbara Holland.[19]

As for quality, there are several ways to improve that as well. Studies unanimously show that turning off all your screens (TV, phone, tablet, computer, and so on) an hour before bedtime can dramatically improve your sleep. Be intentional about your sleep environment by adding blackout shades, lowering the room temperature, and using white noise from a sound machine, phone app, or simply an electric fan in your bedroom.[20] Small changes can make a huge difference, leaving you more refreshed and energized as you climb out of bed.

Practice 2: Eat

The food we eat makes an immediate, long-lasting, and powerful impact on our energy levels. There's a reason athletes are so vigilant about their intake. The best productivity system in the world can't help you if you are starving your body of the nutrients it needs to run at peak efficiency.

Just consider lunch. A 2012 workplace survey by Right Management found just one in five employees gets away from their desks for lunch. Another two in five eat some food at their desks. But almost 40 percent of workers and managers eat lunch "only from time to time" or "seldom, if ever."[21] We can treat lunch like an interruption, but the truth is that it pays big dividends in expanding energy. On the other hand, skipping a midday meal can leave us drowsy, foggy, and fatigued.

Leaving our desks for a meal also pays creative dividends. "Creativity and innovation happen when people change their environment, and especially when they expose themselves to nature-like environments," says Kimberly Elsbach, an expert in workplace psychology at UC Davis Graduate School of Management. She argues that "staying inside, in the same location, is really detrimental to the creative process. It's also detrimental to doing the rumination that's needed for ideas to percolate and gestate and allow a person to arrive at an 'aha!' moment."[22] Missing lunch means you're sacrificing breakthrough moments that could take your organization to the next level in exchange for the unbroken monotony of calls and meetings and spreadsheets and emails.

Of course, the conversation about what does or doesn't constitute a healthy diet could go in a hundred different directions, and all of them are outside the scope of this book. However, I will share a few pieces of advice if you've never made a priority of healthy eating.

First, natural foods such as vegetables, fruits, nuts, and meats are better choices than practically anything you'll find in a package. If you can't pronounce the ingredients or it's loaded with sugar, you might want to think twice. And be mindful when eating out; menus rarely say anything about the quality of the ingredients used.

Second, don't assume you know what a healthy diet looks like if you haven't studied the subject for yourself. The road to poor nutrition is paved with assumptions people make about what are and are not wise food choices. People are too often misled by products falsely advertised as "healthy," "low fat," or other splashy blurbs marketers throw onto packaged foods. The government's recommended eating plan itself has changed over the years, and it is constantly scrutinized, critiqued, and criticized by many health professionals. Knowing what you should eat can be tricky, so do your research and find what works best for you.

Third, be mindful of what you drink. So-called energy drinks, soda, and many other beverages can leave you more depleted than you felt before drinking them, despite the short-term sugar rush you may feel. It's best to stick with water as much as possible.

Fourth, research a nutritional supplement protocol for yourself. Supplements help make up for nutritional deficiencies in our diets. In terms of my personal energy level, I pay special attention to vitamin B_{12} and vitamin D. Both of these play a huge role in helping me manage stress and feel more energetic.

Fifth, it's also important *who* you eat with. Meals are a tremendous way of building relationships. Meals aren't just about refueling. They're about joy and connection as well. Just like spending quality time in bed, spending quality time at the table is key for productivity.

Practice 3: Move

Too often we tell ourselves we don't have enough energy to exercise, but exercise itself is an energizer. It gives more than it takes. In fact, few things have as direct an impact on our energy levels as a decent workout. If you get moving early, it will pay huge dividends all day long.

According to the Centers for Disease Control and Prevention, "Only a few lifestyle choices have as large an impact on your health as physical activity."[23] A regular exercise routine has been tied to weight control, lower stress, vitality, increased energy, reduced risk of heart disease and cancer, and overall improved quality and length of life. Plus, you can achieve these benefits without spending hours a day in the gym. The CDC says, "You can put yourself at lower risk of dying early by doing at least 150 minutes a week of moderate-intensity aerobic activity."[24] That's less than twenty-five minutes a day of some physical activity. Even a brisk walk after lunch can help you take huge strides in improving your health, losing and maintaining your weight, improving your sleep, and boosting your energy levels.

Exercise doesn't just strengthen your body; it strengthens your mind as well. Physical activity primes our brains to op-

erate at a higher level. Writing in the *Washington Post*, journalist Ben Opipari explains, "A single workout can immediately boost higher-order thinking skills, making you more
productive and efficient as you slog through your workday.
When you exercise your legs, you also exercise your brain;
this means that a lunchtime workout can improve your cognitive performance. . . . It improves executive function, a type
of higher-order thinking that allows people to formulate
arguments, develop strategies, creatively solve problems and
synthesize information." And again, this doesn't have to take
a lot of time. Opipari says, "As little as twenty minutes of
aerobic exercise at 60 to 70 percent of your maximum heart
rate is enough."[25]

I don't usually suggest quick-and-dirty hacks when it
comes to productivity, but if you're looking to boost your
mental and physical energy, create a prime atmosphere for
reflection and problem solving, and improve your overall
health all at the same time, try hitting the gym or going for
a run or walk. It works.

High-achievers are notorious for their inability to figure
out how to properly balance their home life and work life.
It may sound crazy, but exercise can make a huge difference
here as well. You might be thinking, "How can adding one
more thing to my already-packed schedule help me balance
home and work life?" That's a great question, and it's one
research has already answered. Russell Clayton, writing in
the *Harvard Business Review*, asserts, "New research . . .
demonstrates a clear relationship between physical activity that is planned, structured, repetitive, and purposive . . .
and one's ability to manage the intersection between work
and home."[26]

People often say they don't have time to exercise. But research shows that people who exercise are actually better at balancing the demands of both work and home than those who skip working out.

Clayton breaks it down to two key findings. First, he explains that "exercise reduces stress, and lower stress makes the time spent in either realm more productive and enjoyable." Second, he notes that exercise creates a greater sense of self-efficacy, the confidence we have in our ability to get things done. Simply put, exercise lowers our stress and makes us *feel* strong, creating a sense that we can conquer the world. That mindset has a huge impact on how we approach both our home and work responsibilities.[27] It carries over into how you approach work, engage with clients and competitors, and view your ability to crush big goals. Maintaining an exercise regimen despite often-overwhelming demands on your time forces you to sharpen your self-discipline and increase your capacity for self-sacrifice. It also helps you hone your efficiency, dedication, planning, and focus to juggle competing interests and opportunities. In short, it gives you an edge in every part of your life.

Demonstrating this point, researchers in Finland followed five thousand male twins for almost thirty years, tracking which were active and which were sedentary. They discovered regular exercise contributed to 14 to 17 percent higher long-term income levels—even between twins who have roughly the same genetic potential. The researchers concluded that exercise "make[s] people more persistent in the face of work-related difficulties, and increase[s] their desire to engage in competitive situations."[28] These traits are directly applicable in a business environment, and they add up to a massive competitive advantage in the marketplace.

Practice 4: Connect

We can't talk about managing energy without talking about the effect other people have on our energy level. The people around us have the power to dramatically boost or drain our energy faster than almost anything else. You can get plenty of sleep, eat a healthy diet, and work out every day, but if you're keeping yourself locked away from other people, not taking the time to invest in quality relationships with friends and family—or worse, hanging out with emotional vampires—you're missing out on one of the most powerful energizers of all.

"The undeniable reality is that how well you do in life and business depends not only on what you do and how you do it . . . but also on who is doing it with you or to you," says psychologist Henry Cloud in *The Power of the Other*. Connecting this observation to managing our energy, he says, "It's not just about managing your workload and taking breaks; it's just as important to manage the *energy sources* around you." Productivity, in other words, is interpersonal.[29]

Dylan Minor, an assistant professor at Northwestern's Kellogg School of Management, demonstrated this point by studying workers at a large tech company. After identifying the high-performers, he analyzed their effect on the people around them. For the coworkers who sat within a twenty-five-foot radius of high-performers, their performance rose 15 percent, which amounted to a $1 million improvement to the bottom line.[30] But as Cloud also says, "People give energy, and they take it away."[31] Minor found "negative spillover" from low-performers could have double the impact high-performers did on profits—just in the wrong direction.[32]

This goes beyond your organization (those you regularly deal with at work) to include your full social circle (everyone you regularly interact with). Your coworkers, colleagues, customers, and clients play a part in your energy management, and so do friends, family members, acquaintances, parishioners, and others—even Facebook friends and Twitter followers. Some of these people come with batteries included, as I heard Dan Sullivan once say. They charge you up. Others don't, and they drain you. Either way, they all impact your energy.

For maximum rejuvenation, you must be intentional about these connections. A night out with friends, a getaway with your family, or a cup of coffee with a colleague can pay back huge dividends in energy and relationship capital over time. Similarly, a disagreeable political exchange with an old college friend on Facebook can drop you in a funk that lasts for hours. Cloud recommends a social audit. Are you surrounding yourself with energy producers or energy drains? Even if circumstances force you into relationships with negative people, knowing the effect they have can prevent the worst of it from rubbing off.

I sometimes hear people say they don't have time for friendships. Overworked people rarely do. Connection is like sleep or exercise in that way. It's essential for high performance, but it's one of the first things we cut when the tasks pile high. For real productivity, however, we need to prioritize people. You are a human *being*, not a human *doing*. Maybe you've forgotten that, but not everything can be measured by check marks on your to-do list. Many of the best things in life happen in the spaces between our tasks, in the intentional moments set aside for other people.

Practice 5: Play

You know the old saying "All work and no play makes Jack a dull boy"? It also makes Jack ineffective, uncreative, unfocused, and unproductive. Never discount the power of play in your life, no matter how many other serious things demand your time. You will always have problems to solve, deadlines to hit, and tasks to finish. That's not going to change anytime soon. If you keep pushing fun to the back burner—maybe to some fanciful vision of a far-off retirement—you'll miss the rejuvenating energy that play provides.

How do I define play? It's activity for its own sake, for fun, for connection with others, or for expressing your own creativity. It's a game like golf or a hobby like painting. It's wrestling with the kids or throwing a ball with your dog. It's hiking outdoors or fishing on a trout stream. It's adventure. It's leisure. It's learning to play the Native American flute (one of my favorites). It's Frisbee at the park, swimming in the sea, and tennis on the court. It's a guitar circle. It's charades, checkers, board games, and jigsaw puzzles. Sometimes

The best things in life will probably never be checked off a to-do list.

it involves challenge and competition. Other times it's just goofing around. Whatever the activity or venue, play is essential to rejuvenation. Because play has no desired end product as such, it flows along on its own. And that's its secret power. When you're not working toward something, you're free to be inefficient, which means you can step back and experiment, try new things, and imagine the world differently than it appears to be. As author Virginia Postrel says, "Play nurtures a supple mind, a willingness to think in new categories, and an ability to make unexpected associations. The spirit of play not only encourages problem solving but, through novel analogies, fosters originality and clarity."[33] Play produces creative breakthroughs.

We all know about the *habits* of highly successful people, but what about their *hobbies*? As psychiatrist Stuart Brown says, "Work does not work without play."[34] The best and brightest already know this. Bill Gates plays tennis. He also plays bridge with Warren Buffet. Onetime Twitter exec Dick Costolo hikes, skis, and keeps bees. And Google cofounder Sergey Brin does gymnastics, bikes, and plays roller hockey.[35] These sorts of activities aren't adjacent to their success. They are part of it. US presidents George W. Bush, Jimmy Carter, Ulysses S. Grant, and Dwight Eisenhower all painted. So did Winston Churchill. "Churchill's great strength," according to historian Paul Johnson, "was his power of relaxation," and painting was a big part of that power. He took up the hobby during a bleak time in his career and kept at it the rest of his life—even through the worst of the Second World War. As Johnson concludes, "The balance he maintained between flat-out work and creative and restorative leisure is worth study by anyone holding a top position."[36]

The key to that kind of restoration, as Churchill himself said, is deviating from our work routines. We use our bodies and minds differently at play than at work. "A man can wear out a particular part of his mind by continually using it and tiring it, just in the same way he can wear out the elbows of his coat," he wrote in an essay on painting, adding an important distinction:

> There is, however, this difference between the living cells of the brain and inanimate articles. . . . [T]he tired parts of the mind can be rested and strengthened, not merely by rest, but by using other parts. It is not enough merely to switch off the lights which play upon the main and ordinary field of interest; a new field of interest must be illuminated.

He went on to say, "It is no use inviting the . . . businessman who has been working or worrying about serious things for six days, to work or worry about trifling things at the weekend."[37] For rejuvenation to occur, it's important to change things up.

That might be one reason time in nature has such restorative power. Taking a break from the busyness of life to engage with nature, even for a few minutes, can bring positive effects for our mental stamina and cognitive performance. In one study, people performing memory and attention tests upped their scores by 20 percent after walking through an arboretum.[38] The time doesn't have to be long. Short "micro-breaks" with nature have discernible benefits for our minds.[39] But long, immersive stretches in nature offer big benefits for our creativity and problem-solving skills. After spending four days in the wild, disconnected from any sort of digital technology, students performed 50 percent better on a problem-solving test. "Our results demonstrate that there is a cognitive advantage to be realized if we spend time immersed in a natural setting," said researchers.[40]

And the positive mental effects don't stop at brainy stuff like focus, creativity, and problem-solving. Nature improves our mood, generosity, and a lot more.[41] Spending time in nature is a great way to find physical rejuvenation. I always feel relaxed when I'm unplugged and outdoors. It turns out the reason is that nature is a stress killer, which offers a cascade of other benefits, including:

- Rejuvenated physical energy
- Reduced anxiety
- Reduced muscle tension
- Decreased stress hormones
- Lower heart rate
- Decreased blood pressure[42]

Many of these benefits rebound to our mental health, of course, forming a virtuous circle. We can look at these benefits like optional add-ons or upgrades to our lives. But the truth is they're normative. We're hardwired to spend time playing, relaxing, and resting, especially in natural environments. If you want to stay sharp, you need regular injections of recreation, exercise, and outright play into your busy schedule.

Practice 6: Reflect

Another source of rejuvenation is reflection. This could take many forms, but most often it's something like reading, journaling, introspection, meditation, prayer, or worship. So much of what we've covered so far emphasizes the body: sleeping, eating, moving, and so on. All of these things are good for the soul. But we also need to spend time intentionally rejuvenating our minds and hearts. This first section of *Free to Focus* is called Stop, and reflection is often the last thing we stop for—if we ever do. But we need to make time for these sorts of reflective practices. If we don't, we run the risk of losing ourselves.

It is so easy for busy people like us to rush through life at warp speed, taking action and making decisions without ever stopping to figure out where we're going, who we're affecting, and what all these actions and decisions are adding up to. This lack of awareness over weeks, years, and decades creates a life lived haphazardly, on the fly, and as a reaction to outside forces. That's not the kind of life you want to look back on.

Along with our frenetic schedules, social media and our instant-gratification culture make this doubly important. It's possible to skip along the surface of our life and never go deeper than status updates, one-click purchases, and streaming television binges. We'll never fully rejuvenate unless we slow down and contemplate our life and the way we move through the world.

Strive to make time for reflection every day. What ideas really matter to you? What are you feeling? Give yourself space to think through your day, including your daily decisions, wins, losses, ideas, insights, and everything else that made the day unique. This exercise ensures that you're connected to a bigger *why* and that you don't get lost in the minutiae of life. Staying firmly connected to your *why* will give you the energy and strength you need to complete your work and finish the race—every day.

Practice 7: Unplug

So how do you win with these practices? It's not an empty question. Even if you buy into them, it can be hard to do them. If we're habituated to overwork, it can be easy to stay connected to our jobs even when we're trying to disconnect. We drift into unhelpful patterns like weekend working and skipping sleep when we should be using our margin to renew our energy. The phone is always in the pocket, the email is a click away, and notifications are pinging and buzzing, demanding your attention.

You could invest in a personal, room-size Faraday cage and shield yourself from any incoming signal. But that might be overkill. Still, we need some sort of way to ensure we unplug. Since this is a struggle for so many, I recommend creating several rules to help you disconnect during nights, weekends, and vacations. Here are four I use (with one exception you'll find in chapter 8). Feel free to create your own and share them with anyone who will help you implement them.

First, *don't think about work*. Put it out of your mind. Preoccupation with work while you're spending time with family and friends makes you physically present but mentally absent. Even when you're there, you're not there. Be mindful of worry creep. When you sense yourself thinking about work, focus on something else instead.

Second, *don't do any work*. This includes staying in touch and up to date. Put your phone on Do Not Disturb, ignore your email and Slack, and shut everything down. You might put your phone in a drawer. Close desktop apps like Slack or email and don't open them during your downtime.

Third, *don't talk about work*. Avoid spending downtime discussing projects, sales, promotions, or work problems. This gives you and your family a much-needed break. Give people around you permission to call foul when you drift back into jobspeak.

Fourth, *don't read about work*. This includes work-related books, magazines, and blogs, as well as things like podcasts and training videos. Cultivate other interests and use your free time to develop passions that aren't work-related.

Next to getting ample sleep, unplugging might be the most challenging of the seven practices. When researchers asked one thousand college students across ten countries to disconnect from their devices for just twenty-four hours, most couldn't do it. "I felt like a drug addict," said one. "I sat in my bed and stared blankly," reported another. "I had nothing to do."[43] That's precisely why the other practices are so important. I'm not suggesting you disconnect from all your devices; that might be helpful, but it's a bit extreme. Instead, I am suggesting filling your rejuvenation time with other meaningful nonwork activities, such as play, connection, and reflection so you fully rejuvenate.

Renewing Yourself

I hope this chapter has blown away some longstanding myths when it comes to managing time vs. managing energy.

Remember, time is not a renewable resource. It is fixed. You can't do anything to add a single second to the day. However, energy is renewable. It flexes, and we can take positive steps to make it flex for our benefit. We can increase our energy exponentially when we sleep, eat, move, connect, play, reflect, and unplug for rejuvenation. Then we can direct that energy however we want, in ways designed to feed our *why*, improve our lives, and lead to the freedom we're all looking for.

Amazing things happen when we Stop. We create space to Formulate, to get a clear picture of where we want to go and what we want our lives to become. We take the time to Evaluate, understanding exactly where we are and what our current situation looks like. And we make the time to Rejuvenate, investing in ourselves and our energy reserves through intentional steps forward in our rest, health, and relationships. It may have seemed counterintuitive to start with Stop, but I hope by now you've seen the value of taking a breath. As we've learned, you can't get where you're going unless you know where you are now and where you want to go. When you've completed the following exercises, you're ready to move on to Step 2: Cut. That's when you'll really start to see your new productivity vision take shape.

REJUVENATION SELF-ASSESSMENT

It can be difficult to make time for things like rest, healthy eating and exercise, relationships, and periods of reflection. But life is better when we make these things a priority. We end up with more energy and stamina, and that ultimately improves every area of our lives—including our productivity.

Download a copy of the Rejuvenation Self-Assessment from FreeToFocus.com/tools. Rank yourself according to the assessment questions and then tally your score. While we often feel tired in general, this tool will identify *specific* areas that may need more urgent attention. Consider retaking the assessment every few months to see how you're improving and what areas still need attention.

Next, download a copy of the Rejuvenation Jumpstart from FreeToFocus.com/tools. This tool will enable you to reflect on a possible goal for each of the seven practices we covered in this lesson. When you've identified at least one goal per area, pick the two you want to focus on for the next month. Finally, to keep your goals in front of you, identify an Activation Trigger for each of those two goals. This is simply something that will remind you about your goal. It could be a note on your bathroom mirror or a reminder on your phone—whatever works for you to remember your goals and prompt the action you need to take.

STEP 2

CUT

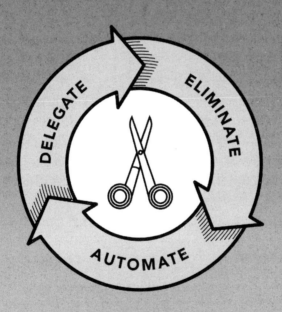

4

Eliminate

Flex Your "No" Muscle

I'm actually as proud of the things we haven't done as
the things I have done.

STEVE JOBS

Several years ago, I put myself through one of the
worst weeks of my professional life. I say "put myself through" because that's exactly what happened:
I said yes to too many things. In one week I attended board
meetings for three different companies, two of which were
out of town. I also had five different speaking engagements
amid the board meetings and travel. Oh, and did I mention
I was also reviewing the copyedited manuscript for one of
my books under a tight deadline? Of course, while I was
running around meeting, speaking, and editing, I dealt with

the 669 emails that came through to my private account. I felt exhausted and overwhelmed, but it was completely my fault. I said yes to all those things.

You've probably had weeks—or months, or years—like that too. Between work, family, social activities, church/community, and a million other types of commitments, we freely give up our precious energy to practically anyone who asks. We know we can't say yes to everyone, but we still take on far more than we should. Why do we do this to ourselves? For many, it's a lack of courage. We may hate conflict, feel guilty about disappointing people, or worry about missing out on new opportunities. Whatever the reason, it is important to get comfortable saying no.

The trick is to remember what's at stake. You've already done the work to figure out your *why*; now you must keep your *why* in front of you all the time. Courage is the willingness to act despite your fear for the sake of an important value or principle. Your *why* is an important value or principle! That means it is worth protecting, and if you don't protect it, no one will.

> I believe courage is the willingness to act despite your fear for the sake of an important value or principle.

If we want to be free to focus, we must eliminate everything standing in our way. That doesn't mean simply saying no to a lot of bad ideas; it also means turning down a ton of good and worthwhile ideas. In today's busy world, staying overworked and overcommitted is easy. The hard work comes in summoning the courage to say no to requests that aren't important and to eliminate those unimportant tasks that are already eating up your time and energy. While other productivity systems focus on constructing the perfect to-do list, I'd rather focus our energy on the road less traveled: the Not-to-Do List.

In this chapter you'll discover how to reclaim your time by eliminating nonessentials—those tasks that destroy your day but don't bring you closer to your goals. We'll attack these time-wasters by reviewing five ways to tactfully delete them from your calendar and task list without wrecking your business. By doing this, you'll learn how to cut out unnecessary tasks and commitments, count the true cost of all your thoughtless yesses, and unleash the power of no. Saying no may sound impossible today, but it's easier than you think. Few things will energize you and your productivity more than the powerful little word *no*. Now let's learn how to use it.

Understand Time Dynamics

Poker isn't known for creating wealth; it's more of a transfer of wealth. It is what's commonly called a zero-sum game. Each player brings money to the table, and that's all the money there is for the game. If five players each bring $100 to bet, then the stakes of the game are $500. That's it. Throughout the course of the game, each player will control a different portion of that $500, but at any given moment, the sum of everyone's holdings will be $500. If they play until "winner takes all," that winner will take $500—no more, no less. Nothing anyone does throughout an entire night of card playing will create more money; all they have to play with is the original $500 from beginning to end.

Even if we hate saying no, we must understand that every yes inherently contains a no.

Time is just like that. It's a zero-sum game. There's only so much to go around because, as we saw in chapter 3, time is fixed. It can't flex. You and I only get 168 hours each week. If time, and therefore your calendar, is a zero-sum game, we must realize saying yes to one thing means saying no to something else. Even if we hate saying no, we must understand that every yes inherently contains a no. For example, if someone asks to meet with me for breakfast at 7:00 a.m., I can't say yes to that without saying no to my morning workout. Or, if I say yes to a client's dinner invitation during the week, I am saying no to dinner with my wife. Do you see how that works? The truth is, even if we hate saying no, we're unknowingly saying no all the time—every time we say yes.

Eventually, all these little yesses and nos add up and we find ourselves with a packed schedule. We get to the point where we can't add one more thing without eliminating something else. That means we must make choices, and these choices are often not between something good and something bad, but between competing opportunities that are good, better, and best.

Acknowledge the Trade-Offs

Yes and *no* are the two most powerful words in productivity. However, we must recognize there is always a trade-off baked into each one. As we saw above, every time we say yes to one thing, we're saying no to something else. It is unavoidable. Time is fixed, remember? I can't accept that dinner invitation from a client and have dinner with my wife at the same time. Even without saying the word *no*, accepting that meeting would mean saying no to the most important person in my life. That's the trade-off for saying yes to the client.

Of course, I'm not saying that these implicit trade-offs are all bad. Just the opposite, in fact. Once you understand the nature of trade-offs, you'll find it easier to say no when you need to. All you have to do is think about the trade-off you're making when you're confronted with an opportunity. Most of us don't do that. We say yes too quickly and only later realize what we've traded in exchange for that *yes*. However, when you go into these decisions understanding you are willfully trading one thing for another, you can exercise control over these decisions. You can knowingly count the cost of saying yes by answering some tough questions. For example, you can ask yourself, *What will I have to give up in order to say yes to this opportunity?* Or, *Will saying no to this allow me to say yes to something better?* Facing these trade-offs head-on is empowering, especially for those who struggle with saying no.

Filter Your Commitments

When examining the trade-offs in our commitment decisions, we need a filter, something that will enable us to process an invitation, request, or opportunity and determine whether we should say yes or no. Wouldn't that make things easier? Just imagine it: a request comes in, we run it through a prepared and familiar decision-making framework, and the right answer suddenly becomes crystal clear. Well, guess what? We already have a filter set up to do exactly that.

In chapter 2 you completed the Task Filter and Freedom Compass worksheets. Like a real compass, it will point you in the right direction. It will remind you of your true north, your Desire Zone, whenever you get lost or start veering off in the wrong direction. As new requests and opportunities pop up and as you review your existing tasks and commitments, here is the rule of thumb you need to cling to for dear life: everything that is outside your Desire Zone is a possible candidate for elimination. I'm not saying all of them should be or will be eliminated, but they're all candidates. If something is outside your Desire Zone, you should at least stop and ask the question, *Could I eliminate this?*

Turning things down and taking things away may not be the picture of productivity you had when you first picked up this book, but now you should know better. You aren't a victim of the *more* myth anymore. You know that true productivity isn't about squeezing more things into your packed schedule; it's about doing the *right* things. That means cutting away the nonessentials is essential.

Think of it like gardening. A good gardener doesn't allow plants to grow wild. Instead, he constantly trims back the plant, cutting off everything that is dead or unhealthy. That's called pruning. The gardener prunes away until only the most robust parts of the plant remain. Why? Because once all the dead weight is removed, the plant can truly thrive and reach its full potential. The same is true for you. By cutting away the nonessentials, you create space for the things that really matter to flourish. Many people get nervous at this stage, but this is where you should have the most fun. Now that you have clarity on how to use the Freedom Compass to guide you, you can begin processing your commitments, projects, and tasks and start the good work of cutting. Best of all, you can do it without fear, because you know you're cutting only those things that are dragging your whole productivity machine down.

One of the fastest ways to get focused on work that drives results is eliminating low-leverage tasks and commitments that fill your lists and clutter your calendar. Cut everything you can from your Drudgery, Disinterest, and Distraction Zones.

Let's start with the things already on your task list. Grab the Task Filter worksheet you started in chapter 2. Now it's time to scan back through your list and see which things you can check off under Eliminate. Here's how: Look at each task on your list that you did not classify as a Desire Zone activity. For each one, ask yourself, *Does this really need to happen? Can I just eliminate it?* For example, if you reviewed your daily activities in chapter 2 and put something like "Surfing the Internet" on your list of tasks, I bet you didn't put that in the Desire Zone. It could be eliminated. Other tasks, however, such as "Vendor Management," may be outside your Desire Zone but still need to get done. In this example, you might not be able to eliminate it, so don't put a check mark there. Don't worry, though. We'll talk about ways to automate or delegate those kinds of tasks later. For now, just check off the obvious things that can be removed with no ill consequences to you or your business. If something could be cut and no one would care, cut it. We'll talk more about how to cut these things later; for now, just be honest and check off the things that ultimately need to go.

Be warned, though. This exercise is going to put a lot of your favorite things—things probably in your Distraction Zone—on the chopping block. Sometimes you must have the courage to tell yourself no too.

Create a Not-to-Do List

I've seen a million to-do list apps and systems, but I've never seen a Not-to-Do List solution. Again, most of the world suffers from the *more* myth, believing the key to productivity is doing more things faster. You've probably tried this approach before too. The problem is, though, the ever-growing to-do list doesn't work. It simply helps us spend *more time* doing even *more things* that ultimately don't matter. That's why so much of the *Free to Focus* system involves pruning.

As I've worked with clients, I've noticed that it can be hard to cut some of these things away. Sometimes we hold on to our "fake work," even when we know better. Sometimes we're fearful of saying no because we don't want to offend or disappoint people. Other times, habit rears its head and we object with a thought like this: "I've always done that job." We slip into what Paul McCartney disapprovingly called a "cozy rut."[1] The work isn't energizing and doesn't help us further our key goals and projects, but we've grown used to it.

The bigger obstacle might be your mindset. I've worked with dozens of people who feel trapped and bored in their work, but they won't make a change because change threatens to destabilize their life. They're focused on what they might lose, not what they'll gain. Too often, we operate with a scarcity mentality that drives us to hold on to things we should abandon simply because we're afraid another opportunity won't come along. Hear me on this: we live in a world of outrageous abundance. The longer I've lived, the more I've discovered this to be true.

I don't really believe in "once in a lifetime" opportunities. There are always more opportunities to be had, and we can't let the fear of missing out lead us into an overpacked list of demands. I mentioned Michelangelo at the start of the book. Do you think he was worried about knocking off another piece of marble when he knew something beautiful and meaningful could be found underneath? No. Besides, if he did make a mistake, he knew he had plenty of other marble to work with on his way to creating a masterpiece. So, don't be afraid to grab a chisel and get to work. You'll never truly thrive as long as you're carrying around the dead weight of your Drudgery, Disinterest, and Distraction Zones.

> We live in a world of outrageous abundance.

Saying No to New Requests

Once you understand that time is a zero-sum game, acknowledge the trade-offs you're making, filter your commitments, and create your Not-to-Do List, it's time to start saying no. Depending on your current list of tasks and commitments, not to mention the new ones that come flying in fast and furious every day, you'll probably have to get comfortable saying no *a lot*. I sure did when I started putting firm boundaries in place. Learning how to say no is a critical piece of your productivity puzzle, so let's spend some time understanding the finer points of a positive no.

"No" is rarely a popular response, but that doesn't mean it must be rude, undignified, or ungraceful. In fact, it's possible to say no in a positive way that leaves both you and the other person better off than either of you were before. There are two common situations in which you'll need to decline graciously. First, you'll need to deal with new requests you haven't answered yet. Those are easier. The second scenario requires a bit more tact and nuance, not to mention a healthy level of personal integrity. These are things you've already committed to that you now know are outside your Desire Zone. There are several strategies for both situations, so let's get started with the requests you haven't answered yet.

No matter how great your productivity system is, nothing can prevent people from making new requests of you. In fact, as you become more productive and efficient, you may develop a reputation for being the go-to person for even more work than ever before. That's why you must develop a bulletproof strategy for gracefully saying no to new requests that are outside your Desire Zone and ultimately aren't worth doing. To help, here are five tips for a tactful no.

1. Acknowledge your resources are finite. Your time and energy are finite resources. We've seen that time is fixed, meaning you can't add to or take away from the hours you have available every day, but what about energy? If it can flex, is it still finite? Absolutely. Even though your energy can flex, it still has limits. You can proactively build up your energy reserves, but you don't have an infinite amount. At some point, you'll burn through all you've got and find yourself exhausted.

If you want to avoid total burnout, you've got to budget your time and energy much like you'd budget your finances. You don't have an endless stream of money coming in every month, do you? Of course not. You can make it flex by working extra hours or landing a new account, but your income still has limits. That's all the money you have to spend for the month, and careful budgeters go into the month with a plan for where every dollar will go. They know that once the money runs out, it's gone. If they run out of money halfway through the month, they must face the fact that some things just won't get done until the next payday. They've exhausted their financial resources. Your time and energy work the same way. You have only so much to spend, so you need to budget for your high-priority items first.

2. Determine who needs access to you and who doesn't. Prioritizing people and projects is one of the biggest challenges for a leader, but it is essential. If you don't carefully budget your time and energy resources, someone else will. They will overrun you with requests and expectations, stealing every minute and ounce of energy from your day. While an open-door policy sounds like a good idea in theory, in practice it can ensure you never get your own work done. Being a good leader does not mean jumping whenever someone calls. Instead, it means focusing on your most important priorities while having systems in place to make sure everything else gets done without you. If you are the go-to person for every project and problem, your system is fundamentally broken. You can serve only so many people well, so make sure you're prioritizing the ones who really need your personal and direct attention.

3. Let your calendar say no for you. One of the best ways to say no is to blame your calendar. You can do this through what's called *time blocking*, and it requires a little intentionality on the front end. When we get into my model for my Ideal Week (chap. 7), you'll see I block chunks of time off for specific high-priority activities. My calendar (and anyone looking at my calendar) sees those blocks as meetings, because they are. I'm scheduling meetings with myself. With my calendar set up this way, I'm prepared to receive incoming requests. When something comes in that doesn't fit my criteria and interrupts my scheduled activities, I simply say I already have another commitment—which is absolutely true.[2]

> I can't accept a new request without going back on a commitment I've already made, even if that original commitment was to myself.

This may be hard for you, so I'll say it again. Even if I am in my office by myself working, I am not lying when I say I have another commitment. I am committed to the high-priority tasks I have assigned myself or have already accepted from others. I can't accept a new request without going back on a commitment I've already made, even if that original commitment was to myself. I consider the trade-off, and I let my calendar say no for me.

4. Adopt a strategy for responding to requests. The best time to plan how to respond to a request is before that request ever hits your desk. You want to adopt a strategy in advance, which will make it much easier to follow through in the moment. Personally, I feel a bit of pressure when someone asks for my time or attention, and if I didn't know from the outset what I would do in these situations, I'd be a lot more likely to give in to the pressure and take on a task I know I shouldn't be doing.

In his book *The Power of a Positive No*, Harvard professor William Ury outlines four strategies for dealing with demands on our time.[3] Three of these strategies do not work, and yet we are all guilty of using them at some point. Only one of the four strategies works, and that one is highly effective almost every time. As we run through each of the four, try to think of a time when you've used each approach.

First is what Ury calls *accommodation*. We say yes when we really want to say no. This type of response usually comes when we value the relationship with the person making the request more than we value our own interests. We don't want to cause a conflict or let the person down, so we accommodate their request.

The second is *attack*. This is where we say no poorly. It's the opposite of accommodation. Here we value our own interests more than we value the importance of the relationship with the other person. Our response to the request is often an overreaction born out of irritation, resentment, fear, or pressure. For whatever reason this request hits us the wrong way, and we attack.

Third is *avoidance*. This is where we say nothing at all. We don't return the call or reply to the email. We act like we didn't see the text. We simply ignore the request altogether or wait a long time before we respond, hoping the situation will resolve itself without us having to get involved. This usually happens because we're afraid of offending the other party, but we really do not want to do what they're asking. As a result, we ignore the problem and hope it goes away. Sadly, it rarely does.

These three bad responses don't work individually, and sometimes they even pile up on each other in what Ury calls the "three-A trap."[4] See if this situation sounds familiar: Someone emails asking for your help with something. You don't want to do it, so you ignore the email (avoidance). A week later they send a second email and make the request again. This annoys you, so you fire back a reply with a harsh or curt no (attack). A couple of hours and maybe an awkward conversation later, you feel guilty for overreacting and reluctantly agree to do what they've asked in the form of an apology (accommodation). That's a vicious cycle of bad responses, and it still ends with you doing the thing you didn't want to do in the first place.

Fortunately, there's a fourth strategy, *affirmation*. This is the response that works, usually creating a win-win for everyone without causing us to sacrifice either the relationship or our own priorities. This healthy response is what Ury calls a "positive no," and it's built around a simple formula with three parts: yes-no-yes.[5] It works like this:

1. **Yes.** Say yes to yourself and to protecting what is important to you. This should also include affirming the other person. You don't want to shame others for thinking of you as a possible solution to their problem.

2. **No.** The answer continues with a matter-of-fact no that is clear and sets boundaries. Do not leave any wiggle room or ambiguity, and do not leave open the possibility that you might be able to do it another time. You

aren't doing anyone any favors by making the person think you might help later if you know you probably won't.

3. **Yes.** End the response by affirming the relationship again and by offering another solution to the person's request. That way, you aren't taking on the responsibility yourself, but you are showing your care and support by helping solve the problem.

This affirmation strategy is surprisingly easy to implement, and it can save you a world of headaches and frustration.

Here's a real-life example of how I use this approach in my daily work. As a former publishing executive, I frequently hear from aspiring authors who ask me to review their book proposals. I get several of these requests every week. I want to honor their hard work and the courage to ask for my participation, but there's just no way I could read, let alone give meaningful feedback to, every request. So I have crafted a response using Ury's affirmation strategy.

First, I begin with a yes: "Congratulations on your new proposal! Very few authors make it this far. Thanks for your interest in having me review it." Then I move to a *no*: "Unfortunately, due to my other commitments, I am no longer able to review proposals. Therefore, I must decline." Notice I didn't leave any ambiguity or suggest I could look at it later if I find time. I set a clear boundary with a firm no. Finally, I wrap up with a yes: "However, I can give you some guidance on how to get published. If you haven't already done so, I recommend you start by reading my blog post, 'Advice to First-Time Authors.' In it, I offer step-by-step instructions for what to do first. I also have an entire audio course called

Get Published, which distills my thirty-plus years of publishing experience into twenty-one learning sessions. I hope you find this helpful." And, of course, I provide links to the blog post and publishing training. I have this saved as an email template so it's always handy and ready to go whenever one of these requests hits my inbox. (I'll share more on email templates in the next chapter.)

Now imagine several situations you regularly face, say a meeting request, a sales offer, lunch invitation, or a part in a new project that's not on your list of priorities. The basic yes-no-yes response can fit them all. Affirm the intent, state why you cannot participate, and then reaffirm. Interestingly, I rarely have anyone pressure me after they receive a response using this formula. They normally reply saying something like, "No problem, I understand. Thanks for getting back to me." I get a negative response occasionally, but that's to be expected. In fact, that leads us to the fifth and final tip for a tactful no.

5. Accept the fact that you will be misunderstood. It is important to prepare yourself for a negative response. No matter how graciously you decline, and even though you may say no for all the right reasons, the occasional person will still be disappointed. Sometimes they will express their disappointment to you directly, which is always uncomfortable. When that happens, though, I politely reply by expressing empathy, but also by restating my no. If you don't respect your own boundaries, no one else will either.

Disappointing some people in life is inevitable, so make sure you're not disappointing the ones who matter most, such as yourself or your family. If I said yes to all those requests to review book proposals, for example, I would never get home in time for dinner with my wife or have time to spend with my children and grandchildren. If someone is going to walk away disappointed, I'm going to do everything possible to make sure I'm not disappointing those closest to me.

Getting Out of Existing Commitments

Now you know how to handle new requests you haven't accepted yet, but what about the things you've already agreed to do? Chances are, you had a long list of existing commitments before you picked up this book, and now you're scratching your head wondering what to do with those things that fall outside your Desire Zone that you've marked for elimination. Let me be clear here: people of integrity keep their word. In other words, if you have already committed to do something, even if it doesn't fit into your new framework, you should find a way to honor your commitment. That said, there is nothing wrong with attempting to negotiate out of the commitment. Besides, if you dread doing something or know it's a poor use of your time, your involvement probably won't be much of a win for the other person, anyway. At best you'll give them minimal effort and attention. That is a good reason to reevaluate the agreement, so let's quickly explore four tips for negotiating out of an existing commitment.

First, *take responsibility for making the commitment.* Don't shift blame or try to play dumb. Sometimes we do this by saying something like, "I didn't know what I was getting into." Even if that's true, you should have clarified the terms before you agreed.

Second, *reaffirm your willingness to honor your commitment*. Do not try to weasel out of the deal you made. This will create a lack of trust not only with the person you're dealing with but also with anyone else who hears about it. Refusing to follow through or help find a solution will damage your reputation, and you want to avoid that.

Third, *explain why honoring your commitment is not the best outcome for the other party*. Focus on what's best for them, not you. No one really cares how this will impact you. All they're likely to care about is the fact that you made a commitment to them and they expect you to fulfill it—and you should. However, if you help them see that your participation may not be in their best interest, they will become more personally invested in helping you find an alternative solution.

Fourth, *offer to help solve the problem with them*. Do not—I repeat, *do not*—shift the burden off your back by dumping it onto theirs. They will resent it, and they will have every right to. Instead, offer to help find an alternative solution. In the meantime, make it clear that you aren't walking out on your commitment until you find a mutually agreeable solution.

Walking through these four steps will ensure you have done everything possible to eliminate the commitment from your list without leaving the other party in the lurch. It will meet their needs and allow you to walk away with a clear conscience and your integrity intact.

Imagine you've agreed to serve on a committee, but now you know you have zero passion and zero proficiency to do it well. It is sitting squarely in your Drudgery Zone. How would you get out of it? First, you might go back to the person and say something like, "I appreciate you asking me to help, but now that I've gotten involved, I realize I made a mistake in accepting this committee assignment." Here you've taken responsibility for the decision you made. You could continue, "Because I made this commitment and you are depending on me, I am certainly willing to honor it and serve out my term." This is your reaffirmation. Then you could explain how your participation could inadvertently hurt the project: "That said, I honestly don't think my involvement serves the committee very well. You need someone who is passionate about the mission and proficient in the area I'm responsible for. Sadly, I've realized that I'm neither passionate nor proficient here, and I think I'm taking up a seat that someone more qualified should have." Then you could move on to the fourth step, offering to help solve the problem. That could sound like, "Would you be willing to release me from my commitment if we could work together to find someone who is better suited for this assignment? I think this would be a win for me, for you, and for this committee."

I have had a version of this exact conversation many times, and I've used these four steps in a wide variety of situations. I'm happy to report I have never had anyone get upset with me. Sometimes they've said no. In those instances I suck it up and follow through with my commitment, giving them my very best effort. That's exactly what they deserve, by the way; it wasn't their fault I made a bad decision, and the consequences should fall squarely on me, not them. But many times the other person has agreed to work with me to find a replacement, and we've all been better off.

Celebrate the Pruning Process

The whole point of this chapter has been to get you comfortable cutting as many things as possible from your calendar. Like a good gardener, it's time to prune your calendar of as many things outside your Desire Zone as possible. When you look at your schedule and to-do list, you want to see only the *right* things. Eliminating means cutting away all the *wrong* things—even if that's 80 percent of your list. Of course, the process of elimination may leave you in an unexpected predicament: you might end up feeling guilty about the time you're freeing up. You may feel like you're letting other people down by saying no when you have time to help them. This is a trap. If cutting out unnecessary or undesirable tasks leaves you with free time or margin, that is something to celebrate! It is certainly nothing to feel bad about.

As Steve Jobs said, "Innovation means saying *no* to a thousand things." Don't give in to the pressure of finding a thousand *other* things to replace the ones you said no to. You aren't making a one-to-one swap as you strike things off your list. As we've said many times, the goal of productivity should be achieving more by doing less. You won't get there if you can't get comfortable *doing less*. Your best actions and best thinking come when you're well rested and you've given yourself the benefit of free time. It inspires creativity and problem-solving like nothing else. So please, make a commitment to free time and don't feel a single ounce of guilt or shame about saying no to activities that are outside your Desire Zone in order to say yes to free time. You'll be so glad you did—and so will the people you love the most.

If cutting out unnecessary or undesirable tasks leaves you with free time or margin, that is something to celebrate!

Take a breath. In the next chapter you'll learn how to automate some of the pesky tasks that are still taking up space on your list.

BUILD YOUR OWN NOT-TO-DO LIST

Time to start eliminating the nonessentials in your life! This is where you start to see your vision of freedom come into focus. Start with your Task Filter worksheet and mark obvious candidates for elimination. Next, download a Not-to-Do List at FreeToFocus.com/tools. Use this worksheet to record the tasks you should *never* do.

Your Task Filter gave you a head start, but don't stop there. Can you think of any others? List the meetings, relationships, and opportunities you should never pursue. Maybe it's a board you need to quit or a report that's outlived its usefulness. When you complete your Not-to-Do List, you should be able to look back at it and recognize each of the items listed as being too low-leverage, unimportant, or irrelevant to occupy your attentions at all.

.

5

Automate

Subtract Yourself from the Equation

Civilization advances by extending the number of
important operations which we can perform without
thinking about them.

ALFRED NORTH WHITEHEAD

f you're like most professionals in the modern world, your
days are filled with questions, demands, requests, pop-in
visits, emails, phone calls, texts, Slack messages, and a
million other distractions from people who want your full
attention. As we've already learned, however, our attention
is both finite and valuable. We can never give everyone our
full attention, and sometimes we can't give them any. If you
want to maximize your productivity, you must identify exactly what does and does not require your attention and, if

something does deserve it, you must figure out *how much* of your attention it deserves. Here's a hint: if it's something that is not in your Desire Zone or one of your high-priority tasks, it doesn't deserve much of your brain power. One method of taking care of critical tasks with little investment of attention is automation. Normally, when I say automation, people assume I mean robots, apps, and macros. But it doesn't take an engineer or a geek to benefit from automation. Every day jobs come up that we don't have time to think about, yet they still need to get done. But who says you have to give the job your *full* attention? What if you could subtract yourself from the equation and still get the job done? That's where automation comes in, and I like to think of the topic under four main headers:

1. self-automation
2. template automation
3. process automation
4. tech automation

In this chapter we'll look at all four and explore several key automation strategies that will enable you to put many of your Drudgery and Disinterest Zone tasks on autopilot.

Self-Automation

Your first step is automating yourself through a process of self-automation. This involves implementing routines, rituals, and habits to make it easier and more efficient for you to follow through on your highest priorities. Again, the focus here is to put as many things in your life on autopilot as possible so you don't have to stop and think about them every time they come up. You want to build rituals and routines so your body knows what to do even if you aren't consciously thinking about it. For example, most people don't have to concentrate on the specific steps involved in taking a shower; they simply know what to do after they turn the water on. Their bodies take over, freeing their minds up to think about other things. That's one reason why we often have such great ideas in the shower. Applying this simple approach to different swaths of your life can be a game changer.

Understanding Rituals. A *ritual* is "any practice or pattern of behavior regularly performed in a set manner."[1] For example, most professional athletes have a pregame ritual, a series of actions that set them up mentally and physically to perform at their best. This is true of high-achievers across all professions. Mason Currey's book *Daily Rituals: How Artists Work* explores the daily rituals of more than one hundred fifty novelists, poets, playwrights, painters, philosophers, scientists, mathematicians, and others. Rituals help these diverse professionals accomplish the same goal we're striving for here: achieve more by doing less. Your daily rituals, says Currey, "can be a finely calibrated mechanism for taking advantage of a range of limited resources: time (the most limited resource of all) as well as willpower, self-discipline, optimism."[2]

Rituals offer three key benefits that set you up to win. First, while many believe rituals squash creativity, the truth is that rituals liberate creativity. Properly formulating rituals requires a tremendous amount of creativity and thought. However, a ritual requires that effort only one time per task.

The goal is to avoid reinventing the wheel every time the same issue comes up. Instead, you focus your creative energy on something once, put a system in place to apply that solution every time, and then you are free to focus your creativity on other things. Consider your daily drive to work. There, you don't have to think about the motions you're going through. Sure, in the first week or two, you had to put a lot of energy into figuring out the best way to the office, how to avoid traffic, and what time you needed to leave. After that initial burst of effort and mental energy, though, the ritual takes over. From then on, your creative juices are free to focus on other things during your drive.

Second, rituals speed up your work. Once you define a ritual, you know exactly what comes next at every step. It's automatic; you simply don't have to think about it, which naturally makes you much more efficient at that task.

Third, rituals correct your mistakes. It might be more accurate to say they *prevent* mistakes, because designing rituals allows you to anticipate different points of possible failure and build in safety nets for each step in the process. Even if you hit a snag early on, you can simply build the solution into your ritual, making the rituals self-correcting over time. Surgeon and medical writer Atul Gawande has highlighted the power of rituals codified in checklists to eliminate error across several industries. He extols the "virtues of regimentation."[3] In his own field, medicine, checklists save thousands of lives and hundreds of millions of dollars every year.

Four Foundational Rituals. You can build a ritual around any repetitive task in your life. In fact, you can create rituals for how, when, and in what order to accomplish a number of different tasks. I utilize and recommend four foundational rituals: morning, evening, workday startup, and workday shutdown. I schedule time for these on my Ideal Week, which I'll cover in chapter 7. By keeping the system running as intended, I'm able to move predictably and efficiently through several necessary actions each day, which keeps my mind free for more hours each day than if I were trying to remember these actions on the fly each and every time I did them.

My morning ritual starts the moment I wake up and carries me all the way into the office each morning. This ritual has nine points, such as "Make a cup of coffee," "Read the Bible," "Journal," and "Review my goals." Together, these nine actions become a routine. I do them the same way, in the same order, every day, which helps me perform them at my best and sets me up for the rest of the day. My evening ritual works much the same way, except it helps me wind down and get ready for sleep. (And here's a pro tip: set an alarm to ensure you go to bed on time.) Everyone's morning and evening rituals will be different, depending on personality, interests, stage of life, and other qualifiers.

What about workday startup and shutdown? These two rituals are clearly marked on my calendar every weekday. My workday startup ritual starts at 9:00 a.m., shutdown at 5:00 p.m. At those two times every day, my brain goes through the motions needed to start or end the workday. I've thought through exactly what needs to happen to get each workday off to a good start and how to end it well, and I put those tasks into a ritual.

As soon as I step into the office, I begin my workday startup ritual. By repeating the same actions in the same order every day, my muscle memory takes over and I can efficiently move through the small set of tasks I need to perform at the start of each day. Again, the list and order of elements will vary by person, but here are the five tasks I need to do to get my workday off to a great start every day:

1. Empty my email inbox
2. Catch up on Slack
3. Check social media
4. Review Big 3 (which we'll discuss in chapter 8)
5. Review my schedule

This ritual usually takes about thirty minutes, so the first half hour of my workday, every day, is dedicated to it. This keeps me from dragging this set of tasks out over the entire morning while I'm trying to focus on other things. It also prevents me from getting derailed by someone else's agenda.

At 5:00 p.m. each evening I begin my workday shutdown ritual. Unsurprisingly, this batch of actions is almost exactly like my startup ritual: email, Slack, and so on. That's because, at this point, I haven't checked email or other messages for about eight hours, and I know I'll need to respond to queries or issues that popped up throughout the day. Since I know I'll be responding more in the evening than I do in the morning, I block off about an hour for the shutdown ritual. If I finish the ritual earlier, I'll go home early. My shutdown ritual includes the same five things as the startup ritual, but I add two more things. First, I review my key weekly tasks and my key daily tasks. Second, I set my next day's key tasks. More on that, by the way, in chapter 8.

Hopefully you are already starting to identify some opportunities for self-automation in your life. It could be a morning, startup, or shutdown ritual like mine, or it could be something altogether different. Perhaps you have a particular way you prepare presentations at work that would be a perfect candidate for automation through a ritual. Once you start looking for opportunities, you will see them everywhere. At the end of this chapter, you'll get started with an activity designed to get your own morning and evening rituals up and running in no time.

Template Automation

In the previous chapter I shared a template I use when budding authors ask me to review their book proposals. That was an example of template automation, and it has been one of my favorite forms of automation for more than three decades. I get requests like this practically every day, and if I had to stop to write a personal, unique email response for every one, I would have no time left to do anything else. Of course, I could hire an assistant just to handle all those incoming requests, but why? Instead, for each one of these things, I spend a little time crafting the perfect response, and then I use that response over and over again. Like we've said before, automation means solving a problem once, then putting the solution on autopilot. Templates let you do this with just a few clicks.

To make templates work, you need to develop a template mindset. Every time you work on a project, ask yourself, *What components of this project will I use again?* If it's something you expect to do more than once or twice, consider creating a template. Even though it takes a little extra effort on the front end, it will save you an enormous amount of time overall.

Automation means solving a problem once, then putting the solution on autopilot.

The most common type of template I use in my everyday work is email templates. You've seen one of these, but trust me, there are more. In fact, I personally have thirty-nine different email templates set up on my computer, ready to go in an instant. My team has embraced this concept, and they have added even more templates to the pile. Collectively, we have more than a hundred email templates we use on a regular basis. If you were to email me or one of my team members right now, there's a good chance you'd get a template-based response. Of course, that doesn't mean it's cold and impersonal. I wouldn't even call it a form letter. Instead, each email template is a thoughtful, personal response to the questions and requests my team is most likely to receive on any given day. It's thoughtful, because we've spent a good bit of time on the front end thinking through our responses. And it's personal, because we build in ways to personalize it to each recipient to make it feel as though it was written just for them.

Now that you know what an email template is, let's explore how I use them. The first step, obviously, is to write a draft of the email. If it's a common email, you probably already have a few different versions of the message saved in your email client's Sent folder. Go back through your old emails and find one that could be crafted into a template. Then write out a new version of the email as though you were responding to a specific individual. Think through all the different ways you could respond and serve the person. In the email I send to authors asking for my help, I was sure to include a link to a relevant blog post I had written and a link to an online training I offer on the subject. I covered all the bases in that draft. That doesn't mean you won't tweak or improve your template over time, but the goal is never having to repeat your high-level thinking.

You might be thinking that the next step is to save the email draft as a document in a folder and copy and paste it into a new email every time you need it. You could do that, but there is a much faster and easier way, and practically any email client will do it. The secret sauce is your computer's email signature feature. I personally use a Mac computer and the basic Apple Mail email client for my email. Like most email apps, Apple Mail lets you save a number of different email signatures. Normally, you'd just use these to automatically insert your name and perhaps your business contact information, but we are going to turn this simple feature into a productivity powerhouse. Once I create a new email template, I save it in my email client as a new signature. Then, when I need it, I can put it into the body of an email in one or two clicks.

In Apple Mail and Outlook, for instance, your saved signatures appear in a drop-down list in a tool bar at the top of the message window. So, when an email request comes in, you can simply hit Reply and choose the appropriate template via email signature from the drop-down list. From there, you can (and usually should) personalize the email with the person's name, but that's about it. What once took ten minutes or more can be knocked out in less than a minute, sometimes in just a few seconds. This is a powerful time-saving strategy for slogging through mounds of email quickly.

Templates aren't just for email, though. You can also create templates of hard-copy letters you send through the mail. For example, if you regularly hire people, you can create letter templates indicating that an application has been received or reviewed. You can even put your digital signature on the document, so you won't have to sign it when you need to send one. Also, if you frequently give presentations using a Keynote or PowerPoint slide deck, you could create a basic template of the slide deck that already has the layout, graphics, and title slides ready to go. However you use templates, the basic concept remains the same: don't reinvent the wheel. Solve a problem once, write it down, and then have it ready to go with just a few clicks whenever you need it.

Process Automation

The third type of automation, process automation, simply refers to a written, easy-to-follow set of instructions for performing a job or sequence. It's similar in some ways to a ritual, but process workflows are generally much more detailed and specific to a set of tasks. Whereas a ritual is more akin to a routine, a process workflow is more like the set of instructions you'd use to assemble a bicycle for your child or a new piece of furniture from IKEA. In those cases, each step of the process is carefully detailed and written, ensuring anyone who can follow directions can successfully accomplish the goal.

I'm sure you can already think of at least one cumbersome process that would benefit from a streamlined, documented workflow. The great news is that they're far easier to create than you can imagine, and their usefulness can't be overstated. Here are five steps to wrangling those annoying, common tasks into one killer process.

1. Notice. The first step in creating a workflow is to pay attention to what you're already doing each week and identify areas where a workflow could help. What actions are key to your business? Which are repetitive by nature? What tasks do you always have to teach someone before you leave town on vacation? What questions have others called to ask you while you were out of the office? What tasks have caused projects to stall because you weren't personally available? Notice the rhythms of your business and note obvious pain points that need documentation. Chances are, you've already thought of several.

For your first workflow, it's best to start with something simple. If you pick your most complicated process to start with, you could get stuck and give up. Set yourself up to win by practicing on a few softball processes first. Once you've picked a simple process to start with, think through the entire procedure from start to finish. Be meticulous in your detail. Visualize everything. I like to assume I'm preparing the workflow for someone who knows absolutely nothing about the work I'm documenting. If I can approach the process as though I were talking to someone completely out of the loop, I can usually capture every step that person would need.

2. Document. Once you know the process you need and you've thought through each part, it's time to write it down. Be sure to capture every step required to complete the task. Don't leave anything out or cut corners. Your goal in this step is to document every little thing on paper so someone who knows nothing about the process could execute it flawlessly. Approach this task like a computer program. A machine will only do what the programmer explicitly tells it to do. It can't fill in the gaps, and neither should the person following your workflow. Give them everything they need to get the job done.

You can document a workflow in many different ways, and it's a good idea to experiment with different formats and tools until you find the ones that work best for you. You can try text-based documentation using a simple word processor or a more advanced note-taking application like Notion or Evernote. Many people include screenshots and screencast videos as part of their documentation, making the workflow drop-dead simple for anyone to follow. And if you want to get especially sophisticated, you could research more customized process-building tools, such as my current favorite, SweetProcess. While software solutions help organize your thoughts and make your workflows pop, don't let tech intimidation keep you from taking advantage of process automation. Even a simple handwritten checklist can get the job done.

3. Optimize. If you didn't cut corners or leave anything out in your documentation, the first draft of your workflow is probably wordier than you'd like. That's okay, because now it is time to optimize. In this step you're going to review what you've written and ask yourself three questions:

1. Which of these steps can be eliminated?
2. Which of these steps can be simplified?
3. Which of these steps should be done in a different order?

By critiquing it in this way, you are fine-tuning the process. You want to give the person following this workflow as much information as they need to do the job, but not so much that they'll skip steps simply because the workflow is too wordy.

This is your chance to streamline the process, making it as efficient as possible.

4. Test. Once you have it written and optimized, it's time to test the workflow. This step is critical. In fact, this is probably where most failed workflows break down. They don't work because the person creating them didn't take the time to test them properly or used their own experience to fill in the gaps where the instructions weren't complete.

In my experience, it's best to be your own guinea pig here. When you test, execute only what've you've written down to see if you've missed anything. *Do not cheat.* If it's not written down, don't do it. Testing what's on the document—and only what's on the document—will immediately reveal any holes or misdirection. Make notes as you go, correcting the workflow until you have a perfect, functioning process document that works as intended, no matter who's following it. You might also ask someone else on your team to test the workflow.

5. Share. Once you know the process document works, it's time to share it with other members of your team via email, with the sharing tools in the application you used to create it, or in a central file server. The point is to share it and to make sure anyone who might possibly need it someday knows where to find it. Don't be surprised if the people using the workflow find gaps. Encourage them to make additional refinements. It won't be long before you've got a flawless process that can be followed by anyone. This is where you see the true power of workflows: they make delegation much more reliable and easier to implement.

The exercises for this chapter include a worksheet called the Workflow Optimizer. This will serve as a handy reminder of the five steps we just covered. For now, though, let's examine the fourth and final type of automation.

Tech Automation

Finally, we come to tech automation—which is what most productivity seekers usually *start* with. Despite the hard time I give technology in this book, such as highlighting the open door it creates for distraction, the positive impact modern software and hardware have had on business is undeniable. I'd argue that automation is at the heart of why we use technology to begin with; we want to offload the heavy lifting and repetitive tasks to a piece of software, thereby freeing our minds up to tackle other challenges. Once you find the right set of tools, it's just a matter of setting them up to run in the background and trusting them to do the job without your effort.

One quick warning as we enter the technology discussion: don't get married to a particular app. Sure, you want to find apps that work best for you, but you should always be open to changing horses if a better, more efficient option comes along—or if your favorite app or service suddenly goes out of business. I've lost count of the number of wonderful apps and tools I've inserted into my workflows that have fallen by the wayside in the endless march of technology.

Over the years I've learned that technology can be counted on, but individual tools cannot. For this reason it's important to focus on the *type* of tool you need more than *which* tool you use. I am always using some to-do list app, for example, because I value that type of software. However, I may change which specific app I'm using at any given time, whether it's Todoist, Wunderlist, Nozbe, or one of the dozen others I've tried. Since type is what matters most when it comes to tech solutions, let's take a look at the four main types of apps that can send your productivity soaring.

Email Filtering Software. Remember when you first discovered email? I do. Maybe you're so young you've never known a world without it, but I remember those early days of email vividly. America Online (AOL) was one of the first consumer-friendly email services, and their trademarked "You've got mail!" message triggered a jolt of joy and anticipation every time I heard it. Today, my reaction to my inbox is much less enthusiastic. Email, left unattended, has become a bloated, demanding beast that could eat up whole days—weeks, even. There have been some weeks in my career I've received more than 700 emails, each one competing for a piece of my limited time, energy, and attention. With that much volume, email has largely become more trouble than it's worth.

If this sounds familiar or hits one of your main pain points, consider investing in some form of email filtering software. We sometimes think of this tool as filtering only spam messages, but that's just the beginning. Good email filtering software helps manage your inbox by automatically sorting through all your messages and filing them into folders based on criteria you set. For example, you could set up filters to send promotional emails, advertisements, newsletters, receipts, personal messages, and project memos into dedicated folders. This keeps them nicely organized from the start rather than adding them to the bottomless pit of a typical inbox.

Most common email services, such as Gmail, Outlook, and Apple Mail, have some filtering functionality built in. Excellent commercial filtering products, such as SaneBox, are also available and are much easier to use. They work like magic, constantly and automatically uncluttering your email in the background. This type of service represents automation at its finest, and I couldn't live in the world of email without it.

Macro-Processing Software. If the term *macro-processing* makes your eyes glaze, stick with me for just a minute. I promise this isn't going to be a lesson on computer programming. Macro-processing refers to software that enables you to batch several small actions into a sequence. This turns many individual micro tasks into a single macro operation that you can trigger with a shortcut key, a text combination, a specific condition on your computer, or even your voice.

I use macros as part of my workflow every day, and mine are tied to keyboard shortcuts. You're probably familiar with using basic keyboard shortcuts such as cmd+C or ctrl+C to copy and cmd+V or ctrl+V to paste. Once you get used to quick shortcuts like that, you almost never reach for the mouse to cut, copy, paste, italicize, or underline text. It's just easier to keep your fingers on the keyboard. That's why I love to incorporate macro keyboard commands into my work. For example, using a program called Keyboard Maestro—Mac only, but there are solutions for Windows—I have several shortcuts set up that will do almost all my common keyboard or mouse tasks. Rather than moving my hands to the mouse or trackpad to find and then launch my mail app, I can simply click a keyboard shortcut to open it. I can do the same to open my other most-used applications.

Opening apps is just the beginning of what I can do with my keyboard shortcuts. I can just as easily trigger much more complex and task-specific actions, many of which have become indispensable to me in my writing. For example, I can highlight a block of text and hit a keyboard shortcut to turn all the selected text into uppercase, lowercase, or title case. This may not be a common need for you, but it is for me. Remember, the first step in automating a workflow is to *notice* what your automation needs are. When I realized how much time I spent mousing over to the different text format options, I decided to invest a little time into setting up macro commands for them. Now I can trigger these things in an instant; it's just part of my muscle memory at this point. Once you set up a macro and train yourself to use it, it can shave tons of time off your workload.

Text-Expansion Software. Text-expansion software is a different type of keyboard shortcut. This is a service that runs on your computer and turns small, defined snippets of text into longer and more complex text. For example, when I type *;f2* into a document, email, or any other text field, my computer immediately expands that shortcut to "Free to Focus™" (including the ™ symbol). Typing the shortcut *;mhco* inserts "Michael Hyatt and Company" into the document. The shortcut *;biz* expands to my local phone number, and *;dlong* expands to the long form of today's date. These are all things I type several times a day, and these shortcuts save me a second here and there all day every day. It adds up.

I even use text expansion for longer, more complex blocks of text, such as replies I commonly use on social media and notes I often send to my team via Slack. Much like my email templates, this allows me to send a personal note in a matter of seconds. I use them so much, it is surprisingly difficult for me to use someone else's computer to get any work done. My favorite text expansion app is currently TextExpander, which is available for Mac and Windows, but several other good options are out there.

Screencast Utilities. Screencast utilities record what's happening on your computer or tablet screen and save it as a video file you can edit and share with others. This type of software is a key piece of my process workflows. In fact, all my online training courses have some level of screencasting. Most computer and mobile operating systems have limited screen recording functionality built in, but professional-grade screencast applications like ScreenFlow and Camtasia take it to the next level. They give you total control of the recording and provide amazing editing tools for post-production. With these higher-end tools, you can overlay a video of your face onto your screen with audio, allowing you to talk to the viewer as you walk them through a screencast tutorial. It adds a huge personal touch to online videos and webinars, and it makes your workflows crystal clear for anyone who depends on them.

Find the Easier Way

In this chapter I've tried to introduce you to the world of automation by reviewing four of the most common types of automation. We started with self-automation, which challenged you to examine your daily routines and build rituals around the things you're already doing (or want to do) each day. Second, we examined template automation, which called you always to ask yourself, *What components of this project will I use again?* This helps you identify repetitive tasks that are ripe for automation. Third, we explored process automation, which is firmly based on documented workflows. And fourth, we dipped our toes in the waters of technology automation as we examined four different categories of tech solutions. I hope these four types of automation have shown you what's possible once you start looking for ways to automate your business and your life.

If you ever find yourself thinking, *There has got to be an easier way to do this*, you should always assume there is. Then go find it. If you apply this question to everything you do on a regular basis, you'll be amazed at how much time, trouble, effort, and energy you can save on all the little tasks that whittle away at your resources. Automating your life will make things easier, free up your creativity, give you greater focus on the higher-leverage activities you need to accomplish, and generally make you more productive every day. Automation is one of the most useful tools in my productivity toolbox, and now it can be one of yours too.

Once you've finished the following exercises, you're ready to move on to the next chapter. There you'll learn how to handle the remaining tasks you can't eliminate or automate by understanding the power of delegation. This one is powerful, even if you don't *think* you have anyone to delegate to. You'll learn tips and strategies that even the most isolated solopreneur can implement immediately, so don't miss it.

STREAMLINE YOUR TASKS

Automation is a powerful force in productivity, but you won't automate your life by accident. You'll only get the time-saving benefits of automation if you take the time to design and implement the systems you want. To do that, I recommend two exercises.

First, download the Daily Rituals worksheet at FreeTo Focus.com/tools. Using this template, you'll design your own four foundational rituals. You'll indicate which activities you want to incorporate and how much time you'll allow for each. Then you'll total those times to see how long it will take you to execute your rituals. The specific activities are entirely up to you, but carefully think through every step you want to include. It may seem weird at first to structure your free time like this, but try it for a month. It will have a life-changing impact.

Next, go back to your Task Filter worksheet. You've already flagged items to eliminate; now, mark candidates for automation and pick one to tackle today. It could be self-automation, template automation, process automation, or tech automation. For process automation, I've got a bonus tool.

Download the Workflow Optimizer at FreeToFocus.com /tools. Note the necessary actions, and isolate and number the steps in the order required to achieve the outcome you want. (Think of it like the ingredients and instructions in a recipe.) Once you've completed a draft, test it and tweak as necessary. You can now reference this workflow to refresh your memory if needed or share it with a team member so he or she knows how to do the job for you—which leads us to delegation.

6

Delegate

Clone Yourself—or Better

I purposed never to do anything that others could or
would do when there was so much of importance to
be done that others could or would not do.

DAWSON TROTMAN

We all know that money can't buy happiness, right?
Well, not so fast. Researchers use the term *time
famine* to describe the feeling of having more
tasks than time. When we're hustling on the wrong side of
the Looking Glass, our lists outrun our hours, and there's
no way to keep up. As we've already seen, the rat race has
a direct, negative effect on our productivity and even our
sense of well-being.

Ashley Whillans of Harvard Business School led a team
of researchers addressing this problem. After studying over

six thousand participants in several economically advanced countries, she found the trick to overcoming time famine and improving feelings of well-being and life satisfaction was simple and straightforward—buy more time. How's that possible?

After you've eliminated and automated as much as possible, you're left with a shorter list of critical tasks that must be done by someone. The question is, *Does that someone have to be you?* Often the answer is no. You can't buy happiness, but you can buy back your time by offloading tasks you deem stressful or unlikeable—and that amounts to the same thing. Delegation boosts well-being by reducing our number of stressful, disliked tasks, and by helping us regain a sense of control over our schedules. "Spending money to buy time was linked to greater life satisfaction, and the typical, detrimental effect of time stress on life satisfaction was attenuated among individuals who used money to buy time," Whillans and her coauthors said of their findings.[1]

Wait, Wait, Hold On . . .

At its heart, *delegation* means focusing primarily on the work only you can do by transferring everything else to others who are more passionate about the work or proficient in the tasks. But let's be frank: sometimes this is hard for high-achievers. Especially if you're cursed with being halfway decent at wearing all the hats in your business. I say "cursed" because it's not a compliment. Would you ever knowingly hire someone only halfway decent? If you insist on doing jobs for which you lack passion and proficiency, congratulations: you win the trophy for worst hiring manager ever.

You can't buy happiness, but you can buy back your time—and that amounts to the same thing.

And we know better. Most of us acknowledge delegation is strategically smart and organizationally sound. The trouble is we view it as an ideal situation that won't work in our specific circumstances. "I have too much responsibility," we might say. "I can't trust someone else to get this done. It's all on me." I've said that plenty of times. But as I tell my clients, who sometimes also say it, it's false. The ultimate responsibility for a task's outcome may fall on you, but you can usually get help with the execution. Similarly we might say, "It's faster for me to do it myself." Again, no. Delegation does require us to slow down long enough to get a new person up to speed. But in the long run, training and trusting others frees up time in our Desire Zone. As Whillans said, it's like buying time.

Some of us refuse to delegate by convincing ourselves we can't afford it. We blame a lack of resources. But as high-achievers, our goals always outstrip our budgets. The main resource lacking in these situations is creativity, not money. Where there's a will, there's a way—whether it's part-time help, a virtual assistant, or an online freelance service. The hours you spend on Desire Zone tasks will always be more profitable than time you're wasting anywhere else, so the cost of delegation pays for itself—and then some. For now,

You can't buy love, but you can buy time. We all get 168 hours in a week. But delegation allows you to redeem some of those hours, especially hours otherwise spent on activity outside your Desire Zone.

don't fixate on resources. You need to get clear on the *what* before the *how*.

The most depressing excuse for not delegating I've ever heard is this one: "I've tried delegation, and it didn't work." If people tried something once or twice and gave up, there would be no art, no music, no technology, no production, no medicine—*nothing*. Imagine a world without art, without music—that is the world of trying something once or twice and giving up. Everything good in our lives is the result of extensive, exhaustive trial and error. If you're letting one or two failures keep you from implementing a major productivity solution, you've got bigger problems than an out-of-control to-do list.

> The main resource lacking in these situations is creativity, not money.

I know it can be tough to let go of tasks you've been personally managing for a long time. But if you want to buy back your time, it's possible, and the results are worth the effort. Pay close attention to the three secrets of master delegators I unpack in this chapter. The first is the Delegation Hierarchy; this will help you get a clear picture of which activities truly deserve your time and energy—and which don't.

The Delegation Hierarchy

To find those key activities only you can or should be doing, filter your remaining tasks through your Freedom Compass. By running through each of the four zones in reverse order, you'll see exactly what tasks need to be delegated off your list and how urgently you need to find a solution for each one. I call this process the Delegation Hierarchy, and we'll start with the tasks you probably hate doing the most.

Priority 1: Drudgery Zone. You'll remember that the Drudgery Zone is made up of tasks you have no passion or proficiency for. Hopefully you've eliminated or automated most of the tasks in this zone. Any tasks left here are prime candidates for delegation—and it's important to hand these activities off as quickly as possible.

When exploring options for delegating your Drudgery Zone tasks, don't feel guilty about handing off your most-hated chores to someone else. Like we saw in chapter 2, just because you hate doing something doesn't mean *everyone* hates doing it. In fact, someone else's Desire Zone could be made up entirely of tasks in your Drudgery Zone. Consider housework, for example. You may dislike cleaning the house and folding laundry, but those things could be at the top of someone else's Desire Zone. Same with accounting, or design, or marketing, or anything else.

I introduced my coaching client Matt in chapter 1. His professional and personal life were transformed when he stopped asking, *Can I do this job faster, easier, and cheaper?* and started asking, *Should I be doing this job at all?* One obstacle for him was delegating Drudgery Zone tasks. "Well, I just need to do it," he would say. "Why would I want to hand it off if I don't enjoy doing it?" It felt arrogant or rude to assign work he didn't enjoy. What changed? "Finding out that my Drudgery Zone isn't someone else's Drudgery Zone. When I'm withholding that assignment, I'm actually keeping people from doing something they enjoy doing." The real arrogance isn't delegating work we don't like; it's assuming everyone likes and dislikes what we do.

Another coaching client, Caleb, discovered something similar. "One particular fear I had was outsourcing a lot of executive support–level tasks, such as responding to customers," he told me. "I was pretty stressed about handing some of those tasks off." Then he started seeing other clients in our coaching sessions succeed with delegation. That gave him the confidence to try it himself. "Having clarity on the activities that fall outside of my passion and proficiency gave me the confidence to hire some executive support staff. A lot of Drudgery Zone activities that weren't giving me any energy are things that give them a lot of energy, and they've excelled at in ways I never could have. By handing that off to them, I've been able to increase my time doing Desire Zone activities from 30 percent to around 70 percent, which has given our business so much more energy and focus and are really the highest leverage activities."

By passing off your Drudgery Zone tasks to someone who loves doing them, you can free up hours per day to focus on things that really matter to you. Plus, getting rid of things you hate doing will give you a new burst of energy you can direct toward your Desire Zone activities.

Priority 2: Disinterest Zone. The next target for delegation is anything that's still sitting in your Disinterest Zone. Just because you're good at something doesn't mean you should do it. Continuing to do tasks you're not passionate about is going to drain your energy from the things you are passionate about.

I know how to do the basic accounting for my business, and I did it competently myself for years. However, I hated doing the job and always put it off. By hiring a CFO who was passionate about keeping the books, I freed up a new block of time for my Desire Zone activities. That's always the goal. So if you're bored with a task that hasn't been eliminated or automated, even if you're good at it, delegate it. It's not as urgent as a Drudgery Zone task, but don't put it off too long. All that boredom will eventually lead to burnout.

Priority 3: Distraction Zone. The tasks that remain in your Distraction Zone after eliminating and automating can be a little tricky. You may be more inclined to hang on to these tasks because you enjoy them, but you also don't want to waste your time or money doing subpar work when a more proficient professional could do the job ten times better.

I enjoy playing around with web design, but my skills aren't nearly what's required to run my business's website. If I tried to manage our website myself simply because I enjoyed it, I would waste an enormous amount of time and the website would break every other day. So even though this one may sting more than others, I encourage you to scrutinize your Distraction Zone activities. Carefully evaluate each task by asking yourself, *To what extent am I passionate about this? Is it worth parking this task in my Development Zone to see if I can hone my skills enough to move it into my Desire Zone?* If the answer is no, delegate it.

Priority 4: Desire Zone. Once you've eliminated, automated, and delegated everything you possibly can from your Drudgery, Disinterest, and Distraction Zones, you'll find your world opens up. It won't happen overnight, but this is the goal—spending most of your time focused on Desire Zone activities. There's only one reason to delegate something in this zone, and that's if your Desire Zone still has more tasks than you can reasonably do yourself. Believe it or not, it's possible to stay in your Desire Zone but still work yourself to death. In fact, it's a real temptation for high-achievers. If you get to this point, you'll need to examine every task and try to figure out which ones you're most passionate about and which ones you're most proficient at. This could lead you to some hard choices about delegating things you love to do. Or at the very least you may find ways to delegate pieces of these tasks, allowing you to keep only the portions you most enjoy and at which you most excel.

Now you know *what* to delegate. But there's more to mastering delegation. Next we'll learn *how* to delegate.

The Delegation Process

Even though delegation is an essential part of leadership and integral to a productive lifestyle, I have seen it fail time and time again. Most leaders may assume they know how to delegate, but when they try to hand a project or task over to someone else, everything falls apart. That failure leaves them not only worse off than they were before, but generally less enthused about trying delegation again in the future. This reluctance drives them to keep hoarding too many responsibilities for themselves, which ultimately drives down their productivity and enjoyment. In the end, the struggling leader is left with an impossible list of responsibilities and little hope that anyone can come alongside to help get it done. Sound familiar?

In a situation like this, it is easy to blame the employee or, worse, assume delegation is an impossible feat altogether. The hard reality, though, is the blame falls squarely on the leader. Specifically, it's because the leader doesn't know how to delegate properly. Many people think delegation is simply a matter of handing someone a task and some instructions, and then reaping the rewards of the other person's efforts. Not usually. Delegation is a process, and it requires an investment of your time. Your goal is to develop passionate, proficient team members whom you can trust with the most delicate tasks, and this will happen only when you walk them through a trust- and skill-building process. If you walk a team member through the seven steps below, you'll not only find yourself surrounded by competent employees, you'll discover untapped leadership potential all around you.

First, *decide what to delegate.* The Delegation Hierarchy shows you exactly what tasks need to be delegated and in what order. Start with tasks in your Drudgery Zone, then tasks in your Disinterest and Distraction Zones, respectively. If you don't have time to do all your Desire Zone tasks yourself, look for ways to trim that list or at least delegate parts of those tasks to others. This step may sound obvious, but this is the starting point. You'll never master *how* if you don't start by identifying *what*.

Second, *select the best person.* The Freedom Compass not only works for you; it works for your team. You aren't the only person who works better in the Desire Zone; everyone else needs to stay in that zone as much as possible too. When you offload a task to someone else, try to find someone with passion and proficiency for the task you're handing off. If you're handing over the reins of your social media accounts, for example, don't pick someone who thinks social media is a waste of time or who has never had a Facebook, Twitter, or Instagram account of their own. They wouldn't know how to maximize your social media outreach, and they wouldn't do a good job at it. That's a recipe for a delegation disaster. To become a master delegator, you must develop the patience and attentiveness to match the task to the person. When you do, you'll set yourself up for unbelievable success.

Third, *communicate the workflow*. Once you've identified the best person, it's time to show them how to do the job. The work you did in chapter 5 documenting workflows can pay off here. Automating your process by creating a documented workflow makes delegation a breeze. Simply hand off the workflow, show them how to use it, and let the system take over. That said, don't worry if you don't have a workflow prepared. Some jobs don't lend themselves to documented workflows. Others may be outside your expertise, making you a poor candidate for identifying all the steps to get the job done. In these cases, just talk through what you need done and the outcome you'd like to see. Depending on the person you chose and the complexity of the task, you may be able to let them try it on their own or document the workflow themselves. Other times you may need to walk them through it once or twice as they learn how to do it. In either case make sure you have clearly communicated the result you need them to accomplish before moving on to the next step.

Fourth, *provide the necessary resources*. In this step you ensure the person who is doing the job has everything they need to follow through and be successful. This could mean providing physical resources like a key, file, or specific tools

for the job. It could mean communicating intellectual resources, such as login information or a piece of software
they'll need. You might also need to provide authorization by
sending an email to the other team members or departments
involved so they know this person will be acting on your
behalf. These are all pesky little details that trip up many
delegation efforts. Carefully think through every step of the
process and make sure that you are handing off everything
they'll need to win.

Fifth, *specify the delegation level*. Before you allow someone to assume responsibility for a task or project, you need to
communicate your expectations. This goes beyond simply re-
laying the step-by-step tactical instructions; it includes being
clear about the level of authority you are giving them. Do you
want them to conduct research only and report their findings? Do you want them to lead the entire project through
to completion without checking in? Each scenario requires a
different level of delegation and failing to clarify how much
authority you are handing off can create chaos and resentment on both sides. A misalignment of expectations can trip
up even the most skilled delegator, so this is an area we will
discuss at length in just a moment.

Sixth, *give them room to operate*. Once the person knows
what they need to accomplish, has everything they need to
do the job, and understands exactly what authority you've
given them to act, you're ready to toss them the keys and
allow them to take over the project or task. This is where
delegation breaks down for a surprising number of people.
While it should be obvious that delegation requires us to
step away and let someone else take over, it can be hard for
us. Sometimes we simply can't make the emotional leap that

enables us to get out of the other person's way. Be careful here; this is where micromanagers are born. I once had a micromanaging boss who made my life terrible. He hovered over me, questioned every action, and second-guessed every decision I made. Nobody should be expected to work under those conditions. If you selected a competent team member and properly prepare them for the task, they'll be able to pull it off. Stand back and let them run with it.

Seventh, *check in and provide feedback as needed*. While you don't want to micromanage, it's a mistake to think you're completely out of the process once you hand the task to someone else. Delegation is not abdication. The outcome is still your responsibility, even if you've outsourced the work to someone else. You'll need to check in periodically to ensure things are progressing the way you want them to. But let me stress again: do not use this as a license to micromanage. Give your team the dignity of doing the job you hired them to do. Just keep an eye on them while they do it until you're sure they have things under control.

Once you've walked a team member through these seven steps, you should expect to see a stream of trustworthy, quality work. As your team members grow, you can give them more and more authority to act on your behalf, and that's when you'll really see your energy and productivity explode.

The Five Levels of Delegation

Part of the Delegation Process we outlined above was to specify the delegation level. This may be a new concept for you, so I want to explain it in detail. Let's start with an example. I recently mentored a young leader we'll call Tom.

Tom was planning a special event, and he was surprised to discover someone on his team had completed a project he didn't authorize. As we spoke, I could tell he was frustrated. He thought his team member had gone way out of bounds, taking more initiative than he was given. After listening to the situation in detail, I finally said, "This isn't your team member's fault. The problem is that you didn't make your expectations clear when you delegated this task."

Tom was stunned. He thought he had been perfectly clear with his employee, but as I walked him through what I'm about to show you, he realized how much confusion and ambiguity he had allowed in the situation. It isn't enough to describe the ultimate outcome you want to achieve when delegating; you also need to specify how much authority and autonomy you're giving to the person. If you don't, you'll be taken off guard by underachievers who do too little and overachievers who do too much. It's your job to let them know exactly how much rope you're giving them. You can do this with the Five Levels of Delegation.[2]

Delegation Level 1. In Level 1 delegation, you want the person to do exactly what you've asked them to do—no more, no less. In this situation, you would say something like, "Here's what I need you to do. Do not deviate from my instructions. I've already researched the options and determined what I need you to do." The phrasing is important here, so let's unpack each part:

- *Here's what I need you to do.* This is where you will explicitly tell the person what you want them to do. No one can read your mind, so be crystal clear.

- *Do not deviate from my instructions.* This creates a hard boundary and makes your expectations clear.
- *I've already researched the options and determined what I want you to do.* This provides the rationale and context for why you've chosen this level.

This level is perfect for new hires, entry level people, contractors, or virtual assistants, or for any other time you're clear on what needs to be done and just need someone to do it.

Delegation Level 2. In Level 2 delegation, you want the person to examine or research a topic and report back to you. *That's it.* In a Level 2 situation, the person you're delegating to will only do research; they won't take any other action on your behalf. This is where my friend Tom messed up in the example above. He thought he was instructing someone to do research and was surprised when the person took action. Tom could have avoided the situation by saying, "Here's what I need you to do. I want you to research the topic and report back with your findings. We will then discuss it, and I will make a decision and tell you what I want you to do." Again, each phrase matters, so let's break it down:

- *Here's what I need you to do.* Be explicit. It's your job to make sure they understand the assignment.
- *I want you to research the topic and report back with your findings.* Clarify what you mean by research at this point. Do you just want them to Google it? Do you want them to conduct an online survey, call several customers, solicit bids from vendors? In other words,

this is where you are clarifying the scope of the research you want done. Clarity is key here.

- *We will then discuss it, and I will make a decision and tell you what I want you to do.* At this point you are setting two critical expectations. First, you're letting them know that you will have a conversation to discuss their findings. Second, you're making sure they know you're the one who will make the decision. This is where you set the boundary that the person is not authorized to take any action or make any decisions.

This is a great level to use any time you're not ready to make a decision and need someone to gather information for you. Once the data is in, you can probably decide pretty quickly.

Delegation Level 3. Starting with Level 3, you're giving the person more room to operate and participate in the problem-solving process, but you are still reserving the final decision for yourself. Here you would say, "Here's what I need you to do. Research the topic, outline the options, and then make a recommendation. Give me the pros and cons of each option, but tell me what you think we should do. If I agree with your decision, I will authorize you to move forward." Let's break it down:

- *Here's what I need you to do.* Be explicit. The same rules apply here as above.
- *Research the topic, outline the options, and then make a recommendation.* Just as in Level 2, be clear about the level and type of research you want them to perform. You're now taking an extra step, though, by asking

them to evaluate the options and actually pick one. You want them to make the decision, but you aren't giving them the authority to implement it.

- *Give me the pros and cons of each option, but tell me what you think we should do.* Here you're asking them to show their work. In other words, they shouldn't expect you to agree with their decision without first giving you the chance to see inside their thought process. This is where they'll explain why they made the decision they did.

- *If I agree with your decision, I'll authorize you to move forward.* At this point it's their job to convince you their decision is the right one. If they can't, their research and arguments are both at fault. If they've done their job well, however, then you can and should give the final approval and authorize them to move forward.

This is a great option for delegating to future leaders you're mentoring, because it gives you a safe opportunity to judge their decision-making skills without any risk. And you probably noticed that this is the level where you start to outsource your decision making. At this stage, you can make a well-informed decision on a complex topic in one simple meeting. What may have taken you a full week can now be knocked out in an hour.

Delegation Level 4. At Level 4, you want the person to evaluate the options, make a decision on their own, execute the decision, and then give you an update after the fact. You would say, "Here's what I need you to do. Make the best

decision you can. Take action. Then tell me what you did."
Sometimes you might want to add, "Keep me apprised of your
progress." You're close to cloning yourself at this point, so the
process should be getting exciting. Let's break this level down:

- *Here's what I need you to do.* Same as above.
- *Make the best decision you can.* You are explicitly
  asking them to make a decision, but they need to put
  the work in first. In other words, they'll do the same
  research as in Level 3, but they're doing it to inform
  their own decision-making process rather than yours.
- *Take action.* Make it clear you expect them to act without waiting on you. This is the first time in the process
  where you've taken your hands off the wheel, so be sure
  it's a person you can trust to act on your behalf.
- *Tell me what you did.* I want to be clear here: This is not
  an opportunity for you to second-guess the decision they
  made. It's done, and there is no going back. This step is
  simply about good communication and keeping you in-
  formed. It also gives you insight into the quality of their
  decisions, which is good to know for future delegation.
- *Keep me apprised of your progress.* This part is optional and is primarily helpful for projects that have a
  lot of moving parts or will take a long time to complete.
  You could even be explicit about the type of updates
  you'd prefer, such as a weekly email or adding it to an
  existing meeting agenda.

This is a great level to use with growing leaders, because
it empowers them with decision-making experience and

gives you plenty of opportunities to evaluate how well they are doing. It's also a useful level for assignments that aren't mission-critical and for which you don't have a strong preference regarding the outcome, such as having your assistant organize and execute Christmas gifts for your clients.

Delegation Level 5. At Level 5, you are effectively handing the entire project or task over to someone else and exiting the decision altogether. You'd say something like this: "Here's what I need you to do. Make whatever decision you think is best. There's no need to report back or tell me what you did." Now you have cloned yourself. This is where you really start to see the benefits of delegation. Let's unpack this last level:

- *Here's what I need you to do.* Same as above.
- *Make whatever decision you think is best.* Like Level 4, you are explicitly asking them to make the decision after doing the research, evaluating the pros and cons, and exploring the best options.
- *There's no need to report back or tell me what you did.* This is really the only thing that makes Level 5 different than Level 4. With this statement, you are releasing them from any obligation to get back to you, and you are officially exiting the process.

Level 5 is where delegation magic happens. It's perfect for when you have complete confidence in the person to whom you're delegating or if it's an assignment that needs to be handled but you really don't care how it's resolved. Examples of Level 5 delegation might be asking your marketing director to decide on a marketing budget for a new product launch or asking your facilities director to replace the furniture in the company break room.

Using the Five Levels of Delegation can transform your personal workload and reduce your stress while also giving your team members ample opportunity to up their own game by progressing through the different levels with you. It's a win-win for everyone. I suggest implementing this process by walking your entire team through the five levels and explaining how you're going to approach delegation from now on. Give them the big picture, and maybe even incorporate the levels by name into your company vocabulary. All of this will work to create a much safer, clearer environment in which everyone knows what responsibility they have in a delegation situation.

Buy Back Your Time

I want to close this chapter with one final word of advice. As I said earlier, people often don't delegate because they think it's faster or easier to do the job themselves. They're right. It is easier to do a single task one time than it is to teach someone else how to do it and walk them through the delegation process and levels. But here's the thing: most tasks are not one-time occasions. These are usually things that pop up often, pulling the leader away from more important work every time. So, while delegation does, in fact, take more time on the front end, it will save you an enormous amount of time every instance after that.

What's more, you'll probably get a better result. Just because you can wear all the hats in the business doesn't mean they all fit. "By delegating and giving people ownership, they can take it to another level," my client Matt told me. "And they can do it a lot better than I was doing. So not only am I not doing it anymore, I'm also getting a better product and the customer is getting a better end result."

The result is that Matt's business is booming. So is Caleb's. For the marginal cost of delegating tasks outside his Desire Zone, he's been able to dramatically impact his bottom line. "My Desire Zone activities are focusing on our clients and ways we can exponentially impact their business," he said. "It's not one of those things you can just check off a list. You really need to have margin and space to be creative." Delegation allowed Caleb to not only serve his existing customers better, it also allowed him to launch new initiatives while still preserving time for rejuvenation.

Time is fixed, but you can buy more. And you will simply never become free to focus on the things that really matter—your top priorities, your key relationships, your most important projects—until you learn how and why to delegate.

In the first section of this book, you learned how to Stop and create a vision for what your life could look like. In the second section, you learned how to Cut by eliminating, automating, and delegating everything outside your Desire Zone. Now it's time to put all these things into action as we move into the final section of this book, Step 3: Act. There you'll learn how to flip the switch on your new productivity machine and get it humming in the background, freeing you up to finally achieve more by doing less. This is the fun part, so knock out this chapter's exercises and get ready for the final push.

PROJECT VISION CASTER

It's time to finish the Task Filter worksheet you've been working on for the past few chapters. If you haven't already done so, download yours at FreeToFocus.com/tools. By this point you've listed and categorized your daily tasks and marked which you can eliminate and automate. Now, what can you delegate? While you won't be ready to outsource every remaining task, you can start to get a vision for where you're going. Delegation doesn't come easy or naturally to most of us; pay attention to any negative voices playing in the background, especially the objections we covered at the start of the chapter.

Next, pick at least one project or task to delegate today. Start by downloading a Project Vision Caster at FreeToFocus .com/tools. This will help you translate your vision for a project or task to paper so your team can see it clearly and execute it with excellence. Use the Project Vision Caster to prepare a team member for the responsibility, carefully choose the Delegation Level that's appropriate, and hand it off. If delegation makes you nervous, don't sweat it. Let the process be a learning experience for both you and your team member.

ACT

ACTIVATE

CONSOLIDATE

DESIGNATE

7

Consolidate

Plan Your Ideal Week

A schedule defends from chaos and whim. It is a net for catching days.

ANNIE DILLARD

When fielding competing demands on our attention, we sometimes default to addressing two or more at the same time. Then we pride ourselves about our ability to multitask. The problem is, the human brain doesn't really multitask. Instead, as journalist John Naish says, "it switches frantically between tasks like a bad amateur plate-spinner."[1]

This kind of switching comes with heavy costs. When you jump between tasks, according to Georgetown computer scientist Cal Newport, "your attention doesn't immediately follow—a *residue* of your attention remains stuck thinking about the original task."[2] Switching isn't seamless. "Attention residue" gunks up our mental gears. One study by the University of California at Irvine found workers averaged twenty-five minutes to resume a task after an interruption like an email or phone call.[3] By breaking our focus, switching also slows our processing ability. When we focus on one task, we filter what's important for the completion of that task. However, when we multitask, we compromise our ability to decide what's relevant and what's not. We start wasting time by processing useless information, and that keeps us in a downward spiral of increasing busyness and decreasing results.

We all develop coping strategies. But if you multiply the impact of attention residue and irrelevant activity over an entire day of interruptions, the costs add up. Have you ever finished a hectic day wondering what you actually accomplished? That's why. We stay busy, but we lose ground on the few things that matter most.

The solution is to design our work to focus on just one thing at a time. The principle is nothing new. Centuries before the advent of smartphones, email, and instant messages, Lord Chesterfield warned his son against the dangers of multitasking. "There is time enough for everything in the course of the day, if you do but one thing at once," he said, "but there is not time enough in the year, if you will do two things at a time."[4] In this chapter we will apply Chesterfield's lesson by learning to consolidate activities to keep your attention where it belongs: on one thing at a time. We'll do this by discussing MegaBatching and your Ideal Week.

The Power of MegaBatching

Most of us have heard about batching. It's the process of lumping similar tasks together and doing them in a dedicated block of time. For instance, you might set aside time each morning and afternoon to empty all your inboxes in your email, Slack, and social media. (You may recall that those actions are part of my workday startup and shutdown rituals covered in chapter 4.) Or you might save a week's worth of reports or proposals to review all at once. Batching is one of the best ways I know to stay focused and blast through tasks. But even dedicated batchers don't always leverage the technique for all it's worth.

Several years ago I started batching on a large scale—what I call MegaBatching. I started with recording my weekly podcast. I used to research and record one new episode a week. It was sometimes hard to drum up the mental energy to produce. What should have taken me an hour or two would sometimes kill an entire day. But I found my team and I could prep in advance and batch record a whole season's worth of shows over a couple of days. Suddenly, I was free from the weekly burden and saved significant time and money.[5]

I found the same thing with meetings. The average professional's weekly schedule looks like a wild, mismatched splatter of meetings. They have no overarching strategy for accepting requests, which allows other people to dictate how they spend their days. But I couldn't afford a calendar designed by Jackson Pollock. When I realized I was the only one who cared about my focus and productivity, I started putting rules around my calendar. Today, with rare exceptions, I batch all my meetings into two days a week. I schedule all my internal team-member meetings on Mondays, and I schedule my external client and vendor meetings on Fridays. That leaves three days in the middle of the week open for intense, focused work without my having to stop what I'm doing to run off to someone else's meeting.

MegaBatching enables me to focus for an extended period on a single project or type of activity, churning out a ton of work quickly and with much higher quality because I'm less distracted. In those dedicated blocks of time, I truly am free to focus on the thing that matters most *at that moment*. This is more than grouping a few things for an hour's worth of work. We're talking about organizing entire days around similar activities to enable you to stay focused and build momentum.

Newport argues that we need extended periods of un-interrupted time to do our best thinking. That's what he calls *deep work*. This gives you the time to immerse yourself in a project and stay there for long stretches of time. What would it look like if you eliminated all those distractions and gave yourself the freedom to focus on one type of activity—uninterrupted—for three hours, five hours, maybe even a few days at a time? MegaBatching enables you to do this. It gets you in the right environment where you can do your best work without having to switch gears. When you reclaim that momentum, you can do your work better, faster, and more enjoyably than you ever imagined.

Because this sort of work is usually done best alone, Jason Fried and David Heinemeier of Basecamp call this time in the "alone zone."[6] I've seen this model popping up in many industries lately. For example, Intel's management created a program to allow their employees big blocks of

You can do your work better, faster, and more enjoyably than you ever imagined.

"think time." During that time, according to *Wall Street Journal* writer Rachel Emma Silverman, "Workers aren't expected to respond to emails or attend meetings, unless it's urgent or if they're working on collaborative projects." She reported, "Already, at least one employee has developed a patent application in those hours, while others have caught up on the work they're unable to get to during frenetic work days."[7] By allowing employees to seclude themselves to focus on important tasks—even if they aren't urgent in the moment—Intel and other companies are reaping the benefits of increased productivity, creativity, and even new product ideas.

That said, it's important to note that collaborative work also yields significant returns when given the appropriate level of focus. MegaBatching collaborative time allows teams to stick with challenges long enough to get the breakthroughs they need to drive results. Whether alone or together, magic happens when we focus on important tasks.

I find it's helpful to divide time across three broad categories of activity: Front Stage, Back Stage, and Off Stage. The metaphor comes from Shakespeare's observation in *As You Like It*:

> All the world's a stage,
> And all the men and women merely players;
> They have their exits and their entrances,
> And one man in his time plays many parts.[8]

The world *is* a stage. It's where we enact the story of our lives. We're players, we have different exits and entrances, and we each play different parts—a dozen different roles any given day if we're not careful. Let's take each of these categories one at a time.

Front Stage. When you think of a stage, you probably imagine the front stage first. This is where the action happens and the drama unfolds—at least from the audience's perspective. An actor's job is acting, and he performs that role on the stage for all to see. The tasks for which you're hired and paid constitute Front Stage activities. I'm talking key functions, primary deliverables, the line items on your performance review. For example, if you're in sales, your Front Stage may be filled with phone prospecting, assessing client needs, or pitch meetings. If you're a lawyer, it might be client meetings, court appearances, or contract negotiation. If you're a corporate executive, it might include presenting marketing plans, leading high-level meetings, or casting a vision for a new product or service.

If it delivers the results for which your boss and/or customers are paying you, that's Front Stage work. It may not be done in public, but Front Stage work enables you to fulfill your work-related calling. That only happens, though, when you have significant overlap between your Front Stage activities and your Desire Zone. The key functions of your job should intersect with where you're the most passionate and proficient.

Your schedule may be so unbalanced right now you can't imagine spending several hours, whole days, or even several days in a row doing Front Stage activities. If so, that's okay; it takes time to apply what we're learning here. But don't let that excuse stop you from moving the right direction. Your Freedom Compass will point the way. You need to be working toward your new destination, even if the path isn't fully clear. You'll find some helpful strategies later in this chapter if you feel stuck.

Back Stage. We primarily see an actor on the front stage, but that's not where he does all his work. Back stage work enables him to step out on stage and shine. The audience sees only the performance; they don't see the initial audition, hours of rehearsals, time devoted to memorizing lines, or rituals an actor performs to produce a good show. For most of us, Back Stage includes step-two activities (specifically, elimination, automation, and delegation) plus coordination, preparation, maintenance, and development. Let's break these down.

You know now the importance of elimination, automation, and delegation, but when will you do it? It takes time to cull lists and calendars, set up templates and processes, and assign tasks and projects. Usually these activities are important but not urgent (more on this distinction in chap. 8). As a result, it's easy to let them go undone for weeks, months, forever. As we've already seen, time invested in these activities will save you countless hours in the long run. The best way to ensure you have the time to invest is to MegaBatch it with Back Stage time. By scheduling time to eliminate, automate, and delegate, you'll get far more accomplished than if you try to squeeze these activities into the margins.

Next, Back Stage work usually includes some type of coordination. This may be as simple as meeting with your team or delegates to plan upcoming projects and tasks. Some meetings, such as an initial vision-casting meeting, may be a Front Stage activity for you, but not all of them will be. Most significant projects take weeks, months, or multiple quarters to accomplish. Once a project is up and running, for example, it will likely require regular check-ins and meetings for accountability, sharing, and collaborative work. That's where coordination slips to the Back Stage.

It also takes Back Stage time to prepare for Front Stage work. An attorney's preparation might include things like poring over case law or rehearsing an opening argument. For a commercial designer, it could be researching color trends or experimenting with lettering techniques for a new logo. For an executive, it might be setting the agenda for a high-leverage meeting or studying the P&L before a financial review. These activities ensure you're ready for a great Front Stage performance.

Maintenance constitutes another key Back Stage task. Nothing can derail your productivity like broken systems, overflowing inboxes, outdated processes, and disorganized spaces. Maintenance includes everything from email management to accounting, expense tracking, file sorting, and tool and system updates—even cleaning your office. Back Stage disorganization can ruin your best Front Stage efforts. Maintenance enables you to put your best foot forward when it's showtime.

Finally, Back Stage work includes time for personal and team development—that is, learning new skills that will enhance and streamline your performances. For an entrepreneur, this might involve attending a workshop to improve public speaking skills or developing a new registration system for webinar attendees. A professional might take a class to brush up on his skills or renew his license. This could also include time most of us spend reading publications about our fields, attending conferences, or investing time to learn new productivity methods. Development is where we make ourselves better, so we can, in turn, perform better on the Front Stage.

However you spend your time Back Stage, it's important to recognize that Back Stage tasks are necessary for Front Stage performance. It's also important to recognize they don't equate to Drudgery Zone, Disinterest Zone, or Distraction Zone tasks. While you're setting aside time to eliminate, automate, and delegate, avoid the trap of using this time to *do* tasks that should be eliminated, automated, or delegated. Back Stage activities will likely be less rewarding and exciting than Front Stage tasks (that's why it helps to be intentional and schedule time for them). But they should not be miserable for you. Remember, the Back Stage makes the Front Stage possible, and all these tasks, wherever they take place, should reflect your passion and proficiency as much as possible. Consult the adjoining table for possible examples of Front Stage and Back Stage work by profession.

Off Stage. This one's easy. Off Stage refers to time when you're *not* working, when you're away from the stage and focused on family, friends, relaxation, and rejuvenation. Off Stage is crucial to restoring your energy so you have something to offer when you come back to the stage (chap. 3). Do whatever it takes to safeguard your time Off Stage.

An actor doesn't live on the stage; he works there. You can't live in your job either. It's a part of your life—a vitally important and rewarding part—but it's not your *entire* life. Balance your time *on* stage with plenty of quality time *off* it. I'll tell you more about how to plan that time in the next chapter.

Examples of Front Stage, Back Stage Work

Occupation	Front Stage	Back Stage
Commercial Artist	Ad design, image editing	Billing, meetings
Marketing Executive	Client acquisition, planning campaigns	Managing budgets, placing ads
Lawyer	Client meetings, mediation	Research, filing motions
Salesperson	Sales calls, pitch presentations	Filing expense reports
Writer	Drafting content, editing content	Emails, research
Executive Assistant	Executing tasks, calendar management	Creating email templates or workflows
Coach/Consultant	Working with clients, developing content	Billing, updating your website
Photographer	Photo shoots, color correction	Billing, equipment maintenance
Owner/CEO	Providing direction, team building	Emails/Slack, meetings
Pastor	Teaching, counseling	Message preparation, board meetings
Accountant	Client meetings, filing taxes	Billing, reading about tax code changes
Personal Trainer	Training sessions, coaching calls	Research, advertising
Financial Advisor	Client meetings, preparing reports for clients	Emails, advertising your services
Store Manager	Team meetings, one-on-ones, hiring	Financial statements, reports
Public Speaker	Speaking engagements, YouTube channel	Message preparation, networking
Entrepreneur	Creating new products, securing clients	Establishing processes, web maintenance
Executive Recruiter	Prospecting, interviewing, networking	Creating templates, organizing contacts
IT Specialist	Troubleshooting, repairs, installs	Research, follow-up, reporting
Real Estate Agent	Showing houses, networking	Paperwork, filing, correspondence

Planning Your Ideal Week

Now that we understand the three categories of activity—Front Stage, Back Stage, and Off Stage—let's harness the power of MegaBatching with a tool called the Ideal Week. This tool allows you to plan your time the way you want to spend it. You've probably heard Dwight Eisenhower's old line, "Plans are worthless, but planning is everything."[9] The workweek is far less dangerous than the battlefield, but a hundred things will militate against your productivity. A plan might not survive the first engagement with the enemy, but having planned, you'll be better able to recover and find your footing. You'll know what you're shooting for.

The premise behind the Ideal Week is that you have a choice in life. You can either live on purpose, according to a plan you've set. Or you can live by accident, responding to the demands of others. The first approach is proactive; the second reactive. Granted, you can't plan for everything. Things happen that you can't anticipate. But it is a whole lot easier to accomplish what matters most when you are proactive and begin with the end in mind. That's what the Ideal Week is designed to do. It is like a financial budget. The only difference is that you plan how you will spend your *time* rather than your *money*. And like a financial budget, you spend it on paper first.[10]

Here's how the Ideal Week works: Think of a completely empty calendar for each day of the week. Most calendar apps will allow you to view a week at a glance, showing each day of the week in seven side-by-side columns. In its purest form your week is a blank slate, and you have the same amount of time as everyone else. How do you want to use it?

You can see how I've structured my Ideal Week in the adjoining example. To create your own Ideal Week, you can download a template at FreeToFocus.com/tools. I also include an Ideal Week template in my *Full Focus Planner.* You could even open your calendar app and create a new blank week or sketch it on a sheet of paper. Don't worry about making it perfect, and don't try to do this on top of your existing calendar appointments. Remember, we're creating an *ideal* week, so let's start from scratch for now. We'll look first at stages, themes, and then individual activities. This progression allows you to take that blank canvas and give it the shape and definition you need to perform at your best.

Stages. The first step is to batch your weekly activities by stage. Decide for each day if you'll be Front Stage, Back Stage, or Off Stage. For me, Mondays and Fridays are Back Stage time; this is typically processing email or Slack messages, organizing files, doing research, learning some new skill or capability, planning future events, or meeting with my team to coordinate projects. These could be whatever days you choose. Think of it as time you are preparing to do what you were hired to do; some days are more conducive to that than others.

The same goes for Front Stage time, which for me is Tuesdays, Wednesdays, and Thursdays. I hold these days for running workshops or webinars, recording audio or video content, and hosting clients, partners, or prospects, individually or (more often) in small groups. As a company, we never hold team meetings on Thursdays; instead, we keep that day open for individual team members to use as they see fit. Many use

Stage	Back Stage	Front Stage	Front Stage
Time	**Monday**	**Tuesday**	**Wednesday**

Themes	Time	Monday	Tuesday	Wednesday
Self	5:00–5:30			
	5:30–6:00			
	6:00–6:30			
	6:30–7:00		Morning Ritual	
	7:00–7:30			
	7:30–8:00			
	8:00–8:30			
	8:30–9:00			
Work	9:00–9:30		Workday Startup Ritual	
	9:30–10:00	Open & Internal Meetings		
	10:00–10:30			
	10:30–11:00		Front Stage Activities	
	11:00–11:30	Support Team Meeting		
	11:30–12:00			
	12:00–12:30			
	12:30–1:00	Lunch meeting with COO	Lunch	
	1:00–1:30		Nap	
	1:30–2:00			
	2:00–2:30	Nap		
	2:30–3:00			
	3:00–3:30	Open & Internal Meetings	Front Stage Activities	
	3:30–4:00			
	4:00–4:30			
	4:30–5:00			
	5:00–5:30		Workday Shutdown Ritual	
	5:30–6:00			
Rejuvenation	6:00–6:30		Dinner	
	6:30–7:00			
	7:00–7:30			
	7:30–8:00			
	8:00–8:30			
	8:30–9:00			

Here's an example of my current Ideal Week so you can get a sense of how to build yours. FreeToFocus.com/tools has additional examples, plus a blank Ideal Week form to use for yourself.

Front Stage	Back Stage	Off Stage	Off Stage
Thursday	**Friday**	**Saturday**	**Sunday**
Morning Ritual			
Workday Startup Ritual			
Front Stage Activities	Open & External Meetings		Church
Lunch			Lunch with my parents
Nap			
Front Stage Activities	Open & External Meetings		
Workday Shutdown Ritual			
Dinner			
Date Night	Family	Friends	Family

it for their Front Stage time. Whatever days you reserve for Front Stage time, remember this is time to do what you were primarily hired to do—that is, the high-leverage work that moves your business, division, or department forward. If you're not getting one to two Front Stage days a week, your performance will suffer.

When planning your Ideal Week, you also want to ensure you're budgeting Off Stage time for rejuvenation. For me this is always Saturday and Sunday. The time might include physically resting, doing something recreational, enjoying long leisurely meals with family or friends, being in church, or building my most important relationships. It is time where I don't work. In fact, I don't even allow myself to think about work, talk about work, or read anything work-related (see chap. 3). Some professionals have different time demands and may need to work outside the typical workweek. That's fine—if you schedule some sort of regular Off Stage time, preferably at least two days a week. If you're wondering how to ensure you take this necessary time off, blocking the time on your Ideal Week is the first step.

Themes. Next, you want to indicate what type of activities you'll do on individual days during certain blocks of time. Don't think about individual activities or tasks right now, just broad themes. An easy way to start is to think of the morning, workday, and evening. I follow this approach and use three themes for my time: *self* in the morning, *work* in the midday, and *rejuvenation* in the evening. Theming the time not only helps identify what you want to do, it also helps you get in the right headspace for the various aspects of your day. Here's how they form the day for me.

Self. I schedule the early morning hours to myself. This includes self-development, working out, prayer and meditation, and so forth. The amount of time you allow here will depend on a mix of your aspirations and your obligations. If you have kids, you might have less time to spare than an empty nester. Regardless, what matters is being intentional with the time you have.

Work. I arrive at the office by around 9:00 a.m., and I quit for the day by 6:00 p.m. Factoring an hour for lunch and a nap in the middle of the day, that is a forty-hour workweek. With the lessons we'll cover in the next chapter, you'll see that's plenty to accomplish my key goals and projects. When will you start and when will you finish? Setting limits on your workday is foundational to productivity. We know from Parkinson's Law that work expands to fill the available time; the lesson for us is that we must limit the availability or it will balloon into the early morning and late evenings. Suddenly you're skipping breakfast and eating takeout at your desk at 7:30 p.m., and as we know from the research on overwork, there's no payoff for those extra hours.

Rejuvenation. I reserve the last several hours of the day for rejuvenation, which includes spending time with my family, friends, and hobbies. You can't bring your best to the rest of the day unless you schedule time to refresh.

You can use whatever labels you want and more than three if that helps. The point is to give clear shape to your day—hard starts and stops—so you know what to expect of yourself throughout. Structuring your day by theme frees you to focus on what's in front of you; be present with who and what needs your attention; be spontaneous, knowing that there's time reserved for work and play; or do nothing at all, which can be very rewarding. Intentional rest and relaxation is key to high performance.

Activities. Once you've identified stages and themes, it's time to group the individual activities that will fall into those themes. As I mentioned earlier, Mondays and Fridays are my Back Stage days, aka meetings, meetings, meetings. By bookending my week with meetings, I'm able to reserve my midweek days for Front Stage activities.

Your Back Stage work might take more days to complete with more variance. What I find with my clients is that the exact time and variance are immaterial if you're intentional about batching as much as possible. Whether it's handling reports, making calls, or preparing a slide deck, batching similar tasks helps you maximize your momentum as you check off the boxes instead of shifting your focus from one thing to the next. Every time you switch and recontextualize—meeting to calls to email to meeting—it slows you down. For Back Stage days, indicate when you'll be available for meetings, when you plan to return calls, and so on.

The exact tasks I do on my Front Stage days (Tuesday, Wednesday, and Thursday) change week to week depending on ongoing and one-off projects, but I always group them as best I can. The trick is to avoid doing Back Stage work during Front Stage time. And that's harder than it sounds. The reality is that you'll have to do some Back Stage work during every day, even if you pare it back to just checking email. The answer is to schedule it and guard against its overflow into your Front Stage time.

I schedule my workday startup and shutdown rituals every day of the workweek, whether it's a Front Stage or Back

Stage day. These rituals include a mix of Front Stage and Back Stage tasks, such as checking email and Slack messages. By bracketing these activities inside rituals and scheduling them two or three times a day, I can prevent task creep. Otherwise, I could be tempted to check Slack periodically throughout the day, opening myself up to a world of interruptions during the most valuable hours of my day. Workday startup and shutdown rituals are a great time throughout the week to process your inboxes, allowing you to get a jump on the day and then close any open loops before you break for the day. If your team requires quicker feedback, you might schedule another inbox check before leaving for lunch.

When it comes to scheduling, resist the temptation to think you can go without breaks. It's possible, but rarely helpful. In his book *Rest*, Alex Soojung-Kim Pang suggests our most productive time each day will amount to four hours, maybe five. His conclusion is based on close study of the work habits of leading scientists, artists, writers, musicians, and others, along with several larger research studies. As you might have guessed by now, longer hours were indicative of low performance. The reason, as we already know, is that time is fixed but energy flexes. We can only sustain concentration for so long before diminished returns set in. The high-performers he studied whose achievements and impact were the most significant worked in focused bursts with breaks for walking, refreshment, socializing, and even play interspersed.[11]

To dial this in, it's worth knowing your chronotype. In his book *When*, Daniel H. Pink highlights what he calls the "hidden pattern of everyday life." We start our day upbeat and energized, but we typically drop into a low-energy trough about seven hours later. For most of us, depending on when you wake up in the morning, that's smack-dab in the middle of the workday. Consider using the trough hours for work that requires less focus. The trough is also a perfect time for a rejuvenating break, even a nap, which can counteract the lull.[12]

The last thing you'll do once you finish drafting your Ideal Week is selectively share it with team members, especially your administrative assistant, so they know when you're available for what. It can also be helpful to share it with supportive supervisors. Since the Ideal Week affects more than the workday, you might also share it with your spouse or others close to you. Explain to them what the Ideal Week is, what you hope to gain from it, and how it will benefit them. You're going to need their buy-in and cooperation to make this work.

A More Productive Rhythm

Lord Chesterfield, whom we quoted at the start of the chapter, viewed single-minded focus as a measure of one's intelligence. "Steady and undissipated attention to one object is a sure mark of a superior genius," he said.[13] I don't know if I'd go so far as to say MegaBatching and planning your Ideal Week will usher you into the ranks of genius—but it's a great start.

Spreading your focus over a million different inputs undermines your productivity, creativity, momentum, and satisfaction. Consolidation—and the focus it provides—offers a better way. By practicing MegaBatching and intentionally structuring your week, you can create the time and space to accomplish goals that otherwise might have seemed out of reach. It's not a matter of genius-level intellect; it's simply a matter of focus and intentionality—two powerful forces that anyone can harness.

Keep in mind that your Ideal Week is just that—ideal. It won't happen every week. In fact, it might not happen most weeks. Life is full of emergencies and unplanned adventures, especially for high-achievers like us. When emergencies pop up, you'll need to pivot. The Ideal Week keeps you from getting disoriented in the process; you know exactly how to get back on track because you already planned it.

That said, once you put firm boundaries in place and force yourself to stay within them for a while, it's amazing how natural it becomes to fall into the weekly rhythm regardless of what's going on. You can think of your Ideal Week like a target. You won't be able to hit the bull's-eye every time, but you'll hit it a lot more often once you know what you're aiming for. Over time, you will be able to use it to guide your work so you become more focused, present, and effective.

How do you adjust for the bumps in the road that throw off your aim? The answer is found in the Weekly Preview. We'll cover that next, along with a simple method for designing your days.

PLAN YOUR IDEAL WEEK

It's time to put some action behind the detailed planning we did in this chapter. Download your Ideal Week template at FreeToFocus.com/tools or use the one in the *Full Focus Planner*. We reviewed the Ideal Week planning process in detail in this chapter, and I bet some of you have already started yours. If you haven't completed it already, be sure to finish sketching out your Ideal Week before moving on. This is the framework you will use next to unlock unprecedented focus in your weekly and daily task planning.

8

Designate

Prioritize Your Tasks

If you don't prioritize your life, someone else will.

GREG MCKEOWN

In the US at any given minute five thousand airplanes are flying overhead, making more than forty thousand flights every day.[1] Air traffic controllers are responsible for making sure they arrive when and where they should without hitting planes leaving the ground. It's tougher than it sounds. One controller described the difficulty of tracking thirty planes at once. "It's like playing ping-pong with 10 people," he said.[2] Every now and then it gets too close for comfort. One pilot complained to NASA's Aviation Safety Reporting System, "We were already close to the preceding aircraft such that we had to fly high on the glide path to avoid wake turbulence,

A key productivity skill is learning to designate what tasks you'll do and when you'll do them. If you try landing every plane at once, you'll create midair collisions that will destroy your most productive efforts.

and they cleared an aircraft on the runway before our arrival that just barely got airborne before we landed."[3]

Aviation officials call that a "loss of separation." It's scary to imagine, but instances are extremely rare, and collisions are even rarer. Compare that with another busy environment—our task lists. We often try landing twelve tasks at once, and projects bump and overrun each other all day long. When we suffer a "loss of task separation" we end up falling behind, making mistakes, and losing control of our time and activity.

Even after you prune your task list in the cutting phase, you still might find yourself facing a huge list of tasks and responsibilities. We are all busy, and we could all come up with an endless list of things that *could* be done. We may even convince ourselves they *should* be done. But do they all have to be done right now? The answer, I'm sure, is no. You never have to land all your planes at once. Just because something is important doesn't mean it's important right now. Of course, you can't defer *all* your tasks for a later time. The trick is to systematically decide what deserves your attention now, what deserves your attention later, and what doesn't deserve your attention at all. In this chapter we'll examine how to stage your tasks by designing your weeks and days. It's about designating what goes where and when. We'll start with the week.

Design Your Week: The Weekly Preview

Leaders and professionals rarely have big initiatives that are accomplished in a single week. Rather, we face complex projects that take several weeks, even months, to complete. Despite our best efforts to maintain focus over the long haul, it's easy to let the beast get away from us. The Distraction Economy may derail you on Monday, and it could be Thursday before you realize how off track you are.

The good news is that you can design your week to keep visibility on your major tasks and review your progress as you go. The trick is to break down your major goals and initiatives into manageable next steps. Then you can map those next steps onto your week by identifying three outcomes you need to hit to make the progress you want. These are the key outcomes that move the ball down the field, yard by yard, toward the goal line. I cover part of this process as it pertains to goals in my book *Your Best Year Ever*. Now it's time to cover it in detail.

The Weekly Preview consists of six steps that will enable you to keep track of all the tasks whizzing overhead and establish a sense of control over your time. You can complete this anytime you want, but it's critical that you do it. The best times I've found are Friday afternoon, as you finish up the workweek; Sunday evening, before the new workweek begins; or Monday morning, first thing as the week begins. My preference is Sunday evening—beyond emergencies that occasionally crop up, it's the one exception I make for my rejuvenation practice of unplugging mentioned in chapters 3 and 7. You should pick what works best for you. Be sure to schedule it as a recurring appointment on your calendar and honor that commitment to yourself. Schedule thirty minutes at first. Once you get used to it, you may find you can knock it out in as little as ten or fifteen minutes. It's just a matter of your personality and the nature of your work.

This process is an opportunity to get your head above the chaos ("ping-pong with ten people") and line up your tasks and action items so they best fit your schedule and responsibilities. This is the key to staying on top of your projects and assignments. The result of a successful week is knowing you did everything you could to keep control of your week, make progress on your big goals and projects, and make your colleagues, clients, family, and yourself happy with your results. Your Weekly Preview should make it clear how well you hit those marks, and it will also ensure you up your game in the coming week. Let's detail the six steps.

Step 1: List Your Biggest Wins. The first thing you'll do in your Weekly Preview is take a moment to reflect on your biggest wins from the past week. List your top accomplishments, the things you're most proud of and that made the biggest impact on your life and work. Be intentional here, even if it doesn't feel natural at first. High-achievers too often focus on their shortcomings—what they *didn't* accomplish—instead of on their wins. That misguided focus can kill your confidence. Focusing on wins instead generates feelings of gratitude, excitement, and personal efficacy and sets you up to tackle big things in the upcoming week.

Step 2: Review the Prior Week. Next, perform a mini After-Action Review. Carefully go through the prior week to recall any lessons you learned and adjustments you should make to see improvement in the near future. You're looking to answer three primary questions. First, *how far did you get on your major tasks from the prior week?* (Here I'm specifically talking about your Weekly Big 3—more on that in a moment.) This is your chance for honest self-reflection. Evaluate your progress on your key initiatives from the preceding workweek. Did you knock them all out? Is there still work to do? (By the way, even if you fall short, you want to give yourself partial credit for the progress you made. High-achievers can be hard on themselves for not accomplishing everything they set out to do and rob themselves of the joy of the gains they made.) Answering this question is important because it plays into the next question.

Second, *what worked and what didn't?* Were there interruptions or distractions you hadn't counted on? What were they? Who caused them? Could you have avoided them? What about your plan? Was it good? Did you budget your time well? The goal here is to note what strategies or tactics were effective and then identify anything wrong with your behavior or planning so you can upgrade your performance the next week.

Third and finally, *what will you keep, improve, start, or stop doing based on what you just identified?* This is where you distill your learning into an actionable lesson. It's also where you give yourself the opportunity to truly grow. How will you adjust your behavior or planning going forward? People who can learn from their experiences and use those lessons to make positive changes in their behavior will advance quickly. Few people take the time to do this, so this can make you stand out from the crowd.

Step 3: Review Your Lists and Notes. Our task lists and daily notes can grow like weeds over the course of a week. It's important to subject these to a quick review so they don't get out of hand. I recommend starting with your deferred tasks. These are tasks you've intentionally decided to bring in for a landing later. If you use a project management tool, you can refer to that for status updates and future planning. As a side note, I also advise keeping your task lists in one place (two places max): for instance, a digital solution such as Nozbe or Todoist, your calendar, or a paper planner. Consolidating your lists will make it easier to keep track of items. The more places you keep tasks and notes the more likely you'll drop balls.

Next, review delegated tasks. These are tasks you've assigned to others. This gives you a chance to put those projects back on your radar and follow up with the person working on them if necessary.

Now scan through your notes from the week. These could be running commentary on your day, observations in meetings, ideas for the future, or other insights you've captured throughout the week pertaining to what you're working on.

People who can learn from their experiences and use those lessons to make positive changes in their behavior will advance quickly.

There will be gems in those lines, and you don't want to drop any good ideas or forget any tasks. To further guard against forgotten tasks, use your review time to take one of the four following actions:

1. *Eliminate.* If a task is no longer relevant, cut it.
2. *Schedule.* If you want to tackle something later, put it on your calendar. Batch similar tasks as much as possible, according to your Ideal Week.
3. *Prioritize.* If you know you want to tackle a task this week but you're neutral on when, prioritize it. Add it to your list of priority tasks for the week, what I call your Weekly Big 3 (hang tight, details coming soon).
4. *Defer.* If it's a task you still want to do, but you don't have time this week, you can just leave it on the list. Keep it on the back burner and consider it again during your next review.

Step 4: Check Goals, Projects, Events, Meetings, and Deadlines. One of the biggest reasons people stumble with their most important goals and projects is they lose visibility. The hectic blur of daily work can obscure even the most important targets and tasks. I mentioned my client Rene earlier. This was her challenge. "It's kind of funny, because I'm in the aviation business," she admitted, "and when you're in the aviation business you think about being at a 30,000- or 40,000- or even 50,000-foot elevation." Unfortunately, Rene spent a lot of her weeks and days in reactive mode. "I used to be stuck in the weeds all of the time. I was grounded."

The Weekly Preview process lets you correct that problem. This is about elevating your vantage point on your work.

Review any goals you're pursuing and reconnect with your key motivations. Just as important, take a moment to identify steps you could take in the coming week to reach your goal. Use this time to also review key projects and deliverables and identify what tasks you *must* do and which you *could* do to complete them.

Now it's time to check your calendar for the coming week (or the next several, depending on what's looming). This is a great opportunity to see if you need to do any preparation, delegate any tasks, or tie down any loose ends before the new week begins. List upcoming events and pending deadlines by date so you can sequence your work. You can't land two planes on the same runway at the same time. It's important to check your upcoming meetings as well; if you need to reschedule or cancel, the more notice you provide, the better.

Step 5: Designate Your Weekly Big 3. Once you've reviewed all your goals, projects, deadlines, and the rest, it's time to get proactive and establish your Weekly Big 3. I define your Weekly Big 3 as the three most important things you need to accomplish in the coming week to keep making progress toward your major goals and projects.[4] I'm sure there are more tasks than you could accomplish in a week, but marathons are finished one stride at a time.

So how do you decide what goes on your Weekly Big 3? One helpful filter is the time-tested Eisenhower Priority Matrix popularized by Stephen Covey.[5] It's a simple grid divided into four quadrants in which the horizontal axis corresponds to urgency, the vertical to importance.

Quadrant 1 indicates tasks that are both important and urgent. These should obviously get the first claim to your time and deserve to be prioritized above everything else. I should also note that *important* and *urgent* mean these things are personally important and urgent for *you*. Too often we get pulled into tasks that are important and urgent to someone else but not necessarily to us. Consider your quarterly goals. How much time do you have left on the clock? What about major deadlines for key projects? Quadrant 1 items should get top billing on your Weekly Big 3.

EISENHOWER PRIORITY MATRIX

As you design your day, prioritize Quadrant 1 and 2 tasks, clear Quadrant 3 tasks quickly (can you delegate any of these?), and eliminate all Quadrant 4 tasks.

Quadrant 2 refers to tasks that are important, but not urgent right now. You can easily defer these tasks, but watch out! Because they're not urgent, Quadrant 2 tasks are often neglected. Then the circling planes run out of gas, and we either cause an emergency or miss an opportunity—or both. When you identify a Quadrant 2 task, also plan to attack it soon.

Quadrant 3 consists of tasks that are time sensitive and important to others, but not necessarily to you. This is where many of us run aground each week. If you aren't careful, you'll allow other people's priorities to supersede your own, derailing your own productivity and stopping progress toward your key goals and major projects. Evaluate Quadrant 3 items on a case-by-case basis. Ask yourself three key questions:

1. If you say yes, are you putting a Quadrant 1 or 2 item at risk?
2. What trade-off are you willing to make to accommodate this new Quadrant 3 request? In other words, what will you have to say no to in order to say yes to this request?
3. Will you end up resenting your participation or the other person if you agree?

If you review these questions and still feel like giving someone else space on your list is a good idea, go for it. However, be careful not to confuse urgency with importance.

Quadrant 4 indicates tasks that are neither urgent nor important to you. Quadrant 4 items should never make it onto our calendars or task lists. But they still do, don't they? I think the reason usually comes down to one of three factors: First, *confusion*. We simply don't stop to evaluate the activity or task. We jump into it without thinking and end up falling down the rabbit hole. Second, *guilt*. We feel like we should do it, even if we know it's not our responsibility. We let guilt override our better judgment. Finally, the *fear of missing out*. We're scared of saying no to new opportunities—whether they make sense in our world or not.

As you designate your Weekly Big 3, don't let other people's priorities crowd out your own. If you really want to be free to focus, you need to set a goal of spending 95 percent of your time on Quadrant 1 and 2 activities. That may seem impossible to you now, but it's not. As you're building your list, ask:

- Is this *important* (to me)?
- Is this *urgent* (to me)?

The answers to those two little questions will build the framework for organizing your priorities and, ultimately, securing your freedom. It made a huge difference for Rene. "My life was driven by my email inbox, not by my goals. That made me feel chaotic and like I hadn't accomplished anything at the end of the day," she said. "I'm a little bit embarrassed to say this as a company owner, but it used to be that I'd get up in the morning and I didn't really want to go to work, but *Free to Focus* has enabled me to pick out my most important tasks and get those accomplished and leave me enough margin to do things that I think are making a difference in the world around me."

Step 6: Plan Your Rejuvenation. Chapter 3 covered this in detail, and we mentioned it again in chapter 7 when discussing your Ideal Week. The Weekly Preview is where the rubber meets the road. Remember the seven practices of rejuvenation: sleep, eat, move, connect, play, reflect, and unplug? Take time here to schedule them into your nights and weekends, or whatever time you reserve for rejuvenation. If you struggle with this, as many high-achievers do, you might want to scan these prompts for each of the seven practices:

Sleep	How much sleep do you want to get each night? What time will you have to go to bed to make sure that happens? What about a nap?
Eat	Are there any restaurants you'd like to try or meals you'd like to cook? (You might combine this with a connection activity.)
Move	Do you want to exercise during your time off? Do you want to try something different than your normal exercise routine?
Connect	Who do you want to spend time with during your time off? What does quality time look like? What activities could you do together to strengthen your connection?
Play	How would you like to play on your time off? Are there hobbies you'd like to pursue, games you'd like to play, or movies you'd like to see?
Reflect	How will you rejuvenate your mind and heart? Reading a book? Writing in your journal? Going for a walk? Attending a worship service?
Unplug	What steps will you follow to ensure you truly disconnect? For example, leave your phone in a drawer; log off work apps; don't think, talk, or read about work.

It's far too easy to drift in and out of our Off Stage time without a plan, but what gets scheduled gets done—including rejuvenation. At the beginning of his journey, productivity for my client Matt was all about getting more done in less time. Using the Freedom Compass and methods like delegation he was able to finally go fully Off Stage. "I'd go into the office pretty much every morning at 6:00 and work till 5:00 or 5:30 and go in a lot on Saturday mornings from about 7:00 till 12:00 or 1:00 to wrap up," he said. Being in the service industry, Matt faced scores of challenges with interruptions. Saturday mornings were his catch-up time. Many of us face that temptation, regardless of profession; we get behind during the week and we use our Off Stage time to tie up loose ends.

Matt put an end to that in his own business. "There are days each week I don't go in to the office. I just stay away, and I shut off my emails on my cell phone. I don't check them at all that day, so that allows me to get focused work done so that I don't have to go in on Saturdays anymore," he said. "Instead of always trying to cram more things into the day by being more productive, I'm now more precise about what I want to get done so I have more time to spend with my family, doing hobbies I love. When I'm at work I'm at work, and when I'm at home I'm at home. *Work hard, play hard,* but separate the two, because it puts a boundary in place."

The Weekly Preview process doesn't take long. As I mentioned above, once you get in the rhythm you can knock it out in as little as ten or fifteen minutes. I included a simple form in my *Full Focus Planner* to facilitate a fast and effective review process. The next part of designating what tasks go when and where is designing our days. There are several elements to consider, but this is a quick process as well.

Design Your Day: Your Daily Big 3

Great days don't just happen; they are *caused.* I spent years going in to the office each day with no real plan in place, simply reacting to whatever happened or filling my time with whatever meeting request or interruption popped up. If that's how you start each day, you are doomed to fail. You aren't taking control; you're *surrendering* control to everyone around you. Your plan can't be to allow everyone else to steer your day or you'll never get anything done that matters to you. Design a day that works for your goals and priorities.

Most of our workdays are filled with two types of activities: meetings and tasks. The combination of these two activities will be different for each of us depending on our job, and each day will look a little different depending on whether we're working mostly Front Stage or Back Stage (see chap. 7).

Meetings represent nondiscretionary time, meaning they are pretty much set in stone the day of. You can cancel the meeting or excuse yourself, of course, but dropping out of meetings at the last minute will cost you relationship capital and put your reputation at risk. Also, you'd be doing a tremendous disservice to the other attendees who might have spent hours preparing for the meeting. That's why it's critical to cover these in your Weekly Preview. If you accepted the meeting and put it into your plan for the day, the only real choice you have is to show up and engage. Occasionally, I will have days that are nonstop meetings with no room for tasks, and you probably do as well. I can see those days coming, however, so I don't plan on accomplishing any tasks then. I also do the reverse: plan days solely focused on tasks and refuse any meeting requests for that day. That's an important step when you know you need uninterrupted time for deep work. Let your Ideal Week guide your planning.

As for tasks, I always shoot for three, and only three, key tasks each day. I call these my Daily Big 3. Now, if this sounds impossible—or even undesirable—I get it. But suspend judgment. If you can get this, it will revolutionize your work, your productivity, and your overall satisfaction level at work and at home.

Most professionals start each day with a laundry list of things they need to do, meetings they need to have, people they need to talk to, projects they need to finish, and so on. Most people set themselves up to fail by trying to tackle too much. It's not uncommon for people to have ten to twenty tasks on their to-do list every day. This is a recipe for disappointment. Even if they accomplish five or six of those, they feel like a failure because that still leaves so many undone.

Stephen, one of my coaching clients I introduced earlier, used to work twelve-hour days, five days a week, and sometimes more. "Six to six were my working days, and even after working that many hours it was stressful not being able to accomplish everything I wanted to get done," he told me. "I was working on a lot of tasks that I don't think I should have been working on, and it just led to more and more frustration and then more and more on the mental desk even outside of work." The overlong hours and mental drain were costing him time—both quality and quantity—with his wife and daughters.

The only solution Stephen had at the time was working harder. "I just kept on pushing, pushing, and pushing, and I thought, *Eventually I'll get there. Eventually I'll start working less.*" But remember the limiting beliefs from chapter 2. "Temporary overwork" is something we say to soothe ourselves about permanent overwork. If you want to stop chronic overwork, make a change: prioritize three and only three tasks.

I find the Pareto principle applies. Following the 80/20 rule, roughly 80 percent of results come from just 20 percent of actions. In my experience, the average person has between twelve and eighteen tasks on their list at any given time. For easy analysis, let's call that fifteen. If the 80/20 rule holds, just three of those tasks are significant compared to the others. Imagine the power of focusing on the 20 percent of actions that drives the 80 percent of results. That's your Daily Big 3.[6]

How do you choose your Daily Big 3? To start with, refer to your Weekly Big 3. Remember, these are the top three outcomes you must achieve for the week if you're going to make progress on your goals and projects. Let your Weekly Big 3 inform your Daily Big 3. These should first be tasks that are in your Desire Zone and other tasks that are in Quadrant 1 or 2 of the Priority Matrix. Keeping your Weekly Big 3 in mind, start with Desire Zone activities, then move on to Quadrant 1 tasks (important and urgent), and finally to Quadrant 2 tasks (important, not urgent). Of course, you'll get outside requests and other tasks that must be dealt with. Follow the Priority Matrix here as well. If you don't, your day will be overwhelmed by Quadrant 3 tasks (urgent to someone else, but not important to you).

> If you want to be free to focus, prioritize three and only three tasks.

Now, this may seem rigid, but it forces you to get laser focused on what matters. It also keeps you from feeling overwhelmed. Why? Because you don't have a long list of things you can't get done. (Who brings their best when they know from the outset they won't win?) Even better, 90 percent of the time, you'll get to the end of the day with everything checked off your list. How awesome would that feel? When you follow this model, you'll see that you're spending every day working only on tasks that are important.

Listing only three tasks for an entire workday may seem like a cop-out, but it requires more discipline and effort than you realize. Writing out a dozen different tasks is a form of laziness, even though the list will keep you busy all day. It takes much more effort to look at the twelve things you *could* do and zero in on the three that *really* matter. And if you think completing only three tasks a day isn't enough to win long-term, consider the year-long implications. If you work five days a week and take off twenty-five days a year for vacations, holidays, and sick time, you'll have 235 working days a year. If you complete three high-leverage tasks each workday, you'll end the year with a track record of 705 completed, important tasks. Can you imagine the impact to your business if you completed 705 important and Desire Zone tasks in a year?

Jim Koch, founder of the Boston Beer Company and brewer of Samuel Adams, built his $1.5 billion business around this simple principle. Writing in *Fast Company*, Koch describes his typical workday. "Each morning I keep myself on track by writing down three to five of my must-do items for the day on a Post-It note," he explains. "These are important, but not necessarily urgent items. Once my day gets going, I keep the list close by as a reminder—it's easy to let these sit or delay and put them off for another day, but I make it a priority to cross them off my list before the end of each day."[7]

The Daily Big 3 works for more than beverages. Ratmir Timashev, cofounder of billion-dollar data management company Veeam Software, keeps his list short as well. "My to-do list is never ending, so it's important for me to prioritize," he says. "Typically, I'll make a daily list of the three most important things I need to get done that day. It really helps to make

my day more manageable. As a morning person, I tend to complete those activities before noon, which then gives me time
to address other urgent items that come up during the day."[8]
Stephen has had the same experience. By focusing on a limited number of tasks, Stephen's working half as much while
growing his business—and he's home around four to spend the
afternoon with his girls. Same with my client Caleb, whom I introduced in chapter 6. "I was overwhelmed and really stressed
about my weeks," he told me. "I always had more on my list
and felt overwhelmed before the day began. I thought, *I'm
never going to get a list down to the Big 3. I've got 20 things to
do today!*" We all do—until we get serious about working in
our Desire Zone and eliminating, automating, and delegating
as much of the rest as we can. That's what Caleb did and it's
paid huge dividends. "It really is possible. Most days I am able
to get clarity on my Big 3 activities. Now that I have a team, I
can delegate other activities to them and focus on those Big 3."
     By focusing on just three key tasks, Caleb has felt a marked
increase in his sense of control. Work is no longer overwhelm-
ing. "It's peaceful. I can't think of a better word than just *it's
peaceful* and gives you so much more energy going into your
workday." Furthermore, because he designed a game he could
win—just three key tasks, instead of twenty random, energy-
draining tasks—he ends the day feeling great about his progress. "I come home in a much better place because I've won."
     Mariel, whom I introduced in chapter 2, also mentioned
the peace that comes from designing her day. "Every morning
I was waking up in a panic attack of all the things that I had
to do that day, and now I'm a calmer and much more peaceful
person. With the systems I've learned, I'm able to know that I
can accomplish what's on my list and walk away from the day

knowing that I've done at least a minimum that will get me toward my goals." Mariel rolled the system out to her whole team, and it's made a difference across the board. "We have an ongoing joke that we don't know how we operated before."

You can keep your Daily Big 3 on a Post-it Note like Koch, in a notebook, or via a task management system like Nozbe. If you struggle with designing your day, the Day Pages of the *Full Focus Planner* can help; that's what I use. But wherever you keep your Big 3, free yourself to focus only on what deserves priority.

Fix the Bounds on Your Time

Seneca, a Roman philosopher who lived around the time of Jesus, wrote about the challenge we all face. "It is not that we have a short time to live, but that we waste a lot of it," he responded. "Life is long if you know how to use it."

We've been struggling with the same issue for two thousand years—and probably a lot longer. We don't guard our time and we squander what we have. "Men do not let anyone seize their estates, but they allow others to encroach on their lives—why, they themselves even invite in those who will take over their lives," Seneca said. "People are frugal in guarding their personal property; but as soon as it comes to squandering time they are most wasteful of the one thing in which it is right to be stingy."[9]

The difficulty is that time is amorphous, and the future doesn't have fixed bounds. The solution is to designate the what and when of our own schedules, starting with the week and then the day. The Weekly Preview, Weekly Big 3, and Daily Big 3 ensure we not only keep visibility on all the potential

"Life is long if you
know how to use it."

—SENECA

tasks we have, they also set hard boundaries around our time. This is a huge step toward defending your time against interruptions and time bandits that will come looking for you.

Now that you've built a layer of defense, it's time to turn our attention to the offense. We'll do that in chapter 9.

DESIGN YOUR WEEK AND DAY

Using the guidelines in this chapter, take the time right now for your first Weekly Preview, including your Weekly Big 3; don't worry if it's the middle of the week. You can download a copy at FreeToFocus.com/tools. You can also find this in the *Full Focus Planner*. Once you're done, set a weekly, recurring calendar appointment with yourself to conduct your Weekly Preview every week going forward.

Next, use your Weekly Big 3 and build your Daily Big 3. Identify the top three tasks that you must accomplish today, and make sure you secure the time to do them on your schedule. I've baked the Daily Big 3 into the *Full Focus Planner* day pages. You can also see a sample at FreetoFocus.com/tools. Commit to the practice of choosing your Daily Big 3 each day for the next several weeks. After three weeks, you should be able to look back on forty-five completed high-leverage tasks that have moved you and your business forward.

9

Activate

Beat Interruptions and Distractions

My experience is what I agree to attend to.

WILLIAM JAMES

Eccentric magazine publisher and inventor Hugo Gernsback was troubled. Even in 1925, there were so many
workplace distractions it seemed impossible to get anything done. To solve the problem, he suggested a new device
called the Isolator. Resembling a large diver's helmet, the
Isolator would block the clickity-clack of office equipment,
the ringing of phones and door chimes, and the chatter of
coworkers. Through two small eyeholes a person could focus
solely on the work in front of him and nothing else—at least
until the oxygen tank ran out![1]

Office disruptions are as old as offices. Inventor Hugo Gernsback created one solution—the Isolator—in 1925! It worked great, until it ran out of oxygen.

As forward thinking as Gernsback was, we live under a barrage of messages and inputs today that would have stunned him. We have social media, texts, app notifications, meeting requests, calls from office phones and mobile phones, and more ambient noise than we can possibly process. The trend toward open-concept offices and cubical farms has worsened this situation for some. What we supposedly gain in collaboration and cost savings we lose in concentration.[2] It's making us so scatterbrained an entire industry has emerged around the practice of mindfulness—the idea that you can shut it all out and just be present. It's harder than it sounds.

The Distraction Economy wants nothing more than to take our minds off what we need to do today. Why? We call it *paying* attention for a reason! Focus is valuable. It's valuable to us, and it's also valuable to others. Every ping that pulls our eyes away and every notification we take note of subtracts value from us and gives it to someone else—e.g., a coworker or an advertiser. And unfortunately, we sometimes make bad trades.

Sure, genuine emergencies pop up, but many of the disruptions we deal with are trivial and unimportant. But even disruptions we recognize as important can be reduced if we know how. When we're focused on our most important projects and tasks, we can't afford to allow interruptions and distractions to derail our days and prevent us from achieving our goals. In this chapter we'll review strategies for minimizing disruptions, maximizing focus, and making sure we can finish each day feeling like we accomplished what we set out to do.

Interruptions: Breaking In

Interruptions represent an external input that breaks your concentration—a drop-in visit, a phone call, an email or Slack message that pulls you away from the work you're supposed to be doing. These are more than mere annoyances. They're cancers gnawing at meaningful work. Even if you manage to complete a task, interruptions ensure that you get to the finish line slower and that the end result falls far short of your best effort. The good news is that you have more power to resist and reduce interruptions than you might think. Two actions can create an effective virtual Isolator to help you maximize your productivity.

Limit instant communication. The speed of communication has accelerated over time. When I first started working, most written communication traveled through the US Post;

a letter typically took several days, maybe a week, to arrive. But then came faxes, emails, texts, and instant messaging. Whereas the phone was once the only means of instant communication, individuals and teams now communicate nonstop in real time via Slack, Microsoft Teams, and other messaging and collaboration apps.

We've confused speed with importance. That mistake has amplified the pace of our communication and the number of our interruptions. A quarter of respondents in one survey said they feel pressured to answer instant messages immediately after receiving them, even if they're working on something else.[3] This has a massive impact on personal productivity.[4]

You can't delve into extended periods of meaningful work if you're constantly shifting your focus when one of seventeen apps or devices alerts you about an incoming message, comment, tag, or desired action. Five years after the iPhone's release, Apple bragged that its servers had delivered over seven *trillion* push notifications. In the years since, the number has only risen.[5] And it's not just your phone. Your computer, tablet, and smartwatch—each with its own ecosystem of apps and widgets and programs—add to the pings and dings and intrusive visuals. Every one of these notifications is designed to capitalize on your attention, which means you can't.

A study by Hewlett Packard and the University of London found when we divert our attention to incoming calls and messages, it dings our IQ by 10 percent; that's twice the effect of smoking marijuana.[6] While it won't permanently impair your cognitive functioning, "it will make you stupid temporarily," say neuropsychologist Friederike Fabritius and leadership expert Hans Hagemann.[7]

The only answer is to opt for delayed communication whenever possible. Unless you work in a customer service position where you have to be "always on," you should engage email or Slack no more than two or three times a day unless you're using those services to actively work on high-leverage projects like your Daily Big 3. I advise using your Ideal Week, along with your workday startup and shutdown rituals, to dedicate time for delayed communication.

	Instant	Delayed
Response expectation	You're already late	You respond at your convenience
Concentration impact	You break your focus	You maintain concentration
Communication depth	Urgency encourages superficiality	Time permits thoughtful engagement
Addiction risk	Dopamine reinforces compulsive engagement	No dopamine hit; no addictive behavior

Turning off your notifications is a critical part of limiting instant communication. I find it's best to start by turning off all notifications—on my desktop, phone, and any other device—and then asking, "Are there any apps from which I absolutely must receive notifications?" Once you've determined which (precious few) apps you'll allow to notify you, you'll want to pick the least obtrusive, jarring alert style possible. For me that means no message previews, pings, dings, or lock-screen notifications. An often-overlooked trick to limit notifications is to make maximal use of your iPhone's do-not-disturb feature.

I also recommend eliminating most text messages and phone calls you receive, especially if you get several dozen (or more) a day. One trick is to change your cell number. It's less of a hassle than it might sound, and it'll be worth it to reduce your interruptions. Along with your new cell number, get a Google Voice number. Only give your new cell number to your immediate family, close work associates, and perhaps a close friend or two. The Google number goes to everyone else: acquaintances, most folks at work, stores, online services, everyone.

Next, download the Google Voice app for your mobile devices. Set it up so that Google forwards text messages and voice mails to your email inbox. You can then process them as you would an email—which you've already cordoned off to a few time blocks each day. You can even reply to a text message email, and it will text the other person.

Set up an automated message in your email program if you want to tell people you only check text messages a couple of times a day. When your email replies with this automated message, they will get a text response. Now the only real-time text messages you get will be from family or those who are in your inner circle.

By limiting your instant communication, you'll experience less stress, more focus, and deep work that will move the needle on your most important tasks and projects. But you can take it even further with one additional action.

Proactively set and enforce boundaries. By opting for delayed communication, you're limiting others' access to you. The trick is to proactively set their expectations by letting them know. Inform the relevant people you're going offline for a period to focus. Don't wait for them to come find you; tell them in advance. You can email or Slack those who need to know. Post a status update in the appropriate channels. Set an autoresponder for your email. Oliver Burkeman says an email inbox is like having a to-do list everyone in the world can populate.[8] Regain and retain control of it by programming your autoresponder to inform others when you're offline and when they can expect to hear back. You can even hang a Do Not Disturb sign on your office door.

Proactively communicating about your availability puts you in charge. Publishing office hours is one way to accomplish this. An open-door policy sounds nice, but you'll never get any meaningful work done if you can't limit incoming access. Setting and announcing office hours keeps you available to your team, but it allows you to plan for those interruptions while ensuring dedicated blocks of time to get your work done.

> An email inbox is like having a to-do list everyone in the world can populate.

What about a boss who expects you to be always on? Your job is to sell your boss on why you need time for deep, focused work. Explain what's in it for them. The more they can see the upside, the greater leeway you'll have to set your own boundaries.

But here's a warning: people will not respect your boundaries if you don't. When someone sneaks past your perimeter defense, be firm and hold the line. If it's a valid request, defer it to a better time. Remember, your time is fixed—so guard it like the precious resource it is.

Distractions: Busting Out

While an interruption is an *external* force demanding our attention, a distraction is anything *internal* that disables or destroys concentration. We're usually our own worst enemies, distracting ourselves from work that needs to be done. When we get bored or when the work we're doing is especially tough, we escape to emails, texts, phone calls, web surfing, checking the news, or scrolling through social media. But every time we bounce off task, we train our brains to become even more distracted and shorten our own attention spans, making it harder to cultivate a life of focus.

Beyond the short oxygen supply, this is why Gernsback's Isolator would never work in real life. As he admitted, "You are your own disturber practically 50 percent of the time."[9] I bet it's more than that. We can blame all the noise and stimuli out there—or we can take the necessary responsibility to change our behaviors.

Breaking Focus. This is the core problem with multitasking. It's not only ineffective, it's an invitation to distraction. One study cited by journalist John Naish found that students were 40 percent slower solving complicated problems when they tried jumping between tasks. Of course, multitasking doesn't feel slow. It actually feels fast, like we're flying. That's part of why we keep doing it, but the feeling of speed is deceptive. Naish cites research that shows multitaskers indeed work faster—but they also produce less.[10]

According to NYU professor Clay Shirky, multitasking "provides emotional gratification" because it "moves the pleasure of procrastination *inside* the period of work."[11] We feel like we're getting things done when we're really dragging them out. If we're drafting an email but then pause to check Twitter, then pull up a newsfeed, then go refill our coffee, and then return to our desk to finish, we've interrupted the thinking necessary to finish the email. It will take us longer to reenter the headspace required to complete the original task. This holds true even when doing similar things but only partially or in a fragmented way. Answering incoming messages while drafting an outgoing message will also lengthen the necessary time.

According to a survey by Salary.com, seven in ten respondents admit to wasting time at work every day, and most use the web. The biggest draw was social media—Facebook leading the pack—but people also reported online shopping and browsing travel, sports, and entertainment sites.[12] How often do we catch ourselves mindlessly surfing from one page to another, or thumbing the infinite scroll on our phones, with no clear objective in mind?

I've heard people say that social media provides breaks in the day, the way people used to walk or go outdoors for a smoke. That's part of what's happening, but the accessibility of social media means people aren't usually working for a long period and then taking a break. They're breaking their concentration multiple times in what Cal Newport calls "quick checks" during the working period. Instead of taking a break, they're breaking their focus.

Doing Downhill Work. A lot of this has to do with low frustration tolerance. In their book *The Distracted Mind*, professors Adam Gazzaley and Larry Rosen say humans are inherently attention-seeking. When we get bored, anxious, or uncomfortable, it's easy to *change the channel* instantly to find something more interesting. Gazzaley and Rosen cite a study of Stanford students whose computers were set to take screenshots of their activity throughout the day. The students rarely stayed on one screen for long. In fact, their attention lasted for about a minute on average—but half of the switches happened after only nineteen seconds.

What's even more interesting, though, is what was happening in their brains during the switches. Sensors attached to the test subjects picked up elevated levels of arousal several seconds before the student switched to something else— especially when the students switched from a difficult task like writing and research to something more entertaining like social media or YouTube.[13]

Professionals are guilty of this too. When we get stumped on something tough, it's tempting to give our brains a rest by switching to something more enjoyable. Think of an incline. It's easier to go downhill than up. Some tasks are uphill tasks (say, financial analysis or writing) and others downhill (say, checking email or Slack). The uphill tasks are usually the ones that drive results and create value in our organizations. But the downhill tasks demand less energy. That's one of the reasons people do so much fake work; it's easier. There's almost a gravitational pull to it. But there's a huge productivity cost for getting distracted by downhill tasks when we need to focus on going uphill.

If you're working on a challenging task and jump off to check email or Slack, it takes extra time and energy to get back to the original task. Jumping off the hard task is easy; jumping off the easy task is hard. It demands even more energy than simply sticking with the uphill task.[14] That's in the short run. The long-run productivity costs are even higher. When we bail on uphill tasks too soon, it creates a pattern in which it gets harder and harder to stick with a difficult task before bailing. Switching from uphill tasks to downhill tasks (or worse, nontasks like Facebook) triggers a dopamine hit in our brains. This registers as a pleasurable reward for our behavior. We get a rush of relief when we allow ourselves to switch off from a difficult task on to something easier. This makes it harder to return to work, which makes it even easier to bail next time. This insidious cycle—which is the same driver for any addictive behavior—incrementally shrinks our attention span. It's like self-induced Attention Deficit Disorder. In fact, ADD specialist Edward Hallowell calls this learned habit Attention Deficit Trait and says it's "everywhere, especially at work."[15]

Focus Tactics

If we want to get free to focus, we don't need Gernsback's Isolator. Instead, we need tactics to help us regain, retain, and ultimately retrain our focus. You're already getting enough sleep (chap. 3) and disengaging from instant communication. Both of those help. Here are some additional suggestions:

Use technology to manage technology. If you Google "focus applications," you'll see a new wave of software apps designed to minimize distractions online. I'm currently using one called Freedom, which is cross-platform and highly customizable. It allows you to customize what apps and websites you can access during dedicated periods of deep work.

When we get stumped on something tough, it's tempting to give our brains a rest by switching to something more enjoyable.

For example, because I do so much online research, I can't work well without the internet. However, I can use Freedom to temporarily block Facebook, Twitter, news sites, and other noisy apps I don't need at the moment. It's a great tool, and there are several others like it. After using it for a while, you'll be surprised how much it curtails your compulsive habits on your phone and computer.

Listen to the right music. Listening to music might seem counterproductive when you're trying to focus, especially if you're exerting mental energy to screen out annoying jingles or expending effort to process lyrics when your brain is busy on more important matters. But there are some helpful ways to use it to your advantage.

Background music that's familiar, repetitive, relatively simple, and not too loud can aid focus, and there's good evidence that upbeat classical music can help with creative work.[16] Some even recommend video game soundtracks. But there's no perfect or ideal style; it mostly comes down to individual preference. "Music you like increases focus," says neuroscientist Dean Burnett, "while music you don't impedes it."[17] For me, that's Baroque music (such as Bach, Handel, or Telemann) and movie soundtracks. Music is also useful for masking workplace noise, but you need to ensure it doesn't become its own distraction.

I listen to music whenever I want to get out of the world and into my work. Focus@Will is an online service like Pandora but one that streams music selected specifically to lengthen your attention span and improve your concentration. And Focus@Will also lets you set up time-bound work sessions.

Take charge of your environment. Make your workspace
work for you. If you find your environment distracting, consider changing the scenery. Variety can reenergize us and facilitate deep work. This is easy if you work remotely, but even office workers have more flexibility here than they might realize.

I worked with an editor who would relocate from his office
whenever he had marathon editing sessions: a table on the
patio outdoors, an empty conference room, or a corner in the
cafeteria during a lull in the lunchtime traffic. He couldn't
stand coffee shops but knocked out one book after another in
a nearby cigar shop. The trick is to find an environment that
works for you.[18] In his book *Willpower Doesn't Work*, Benjamin Hardy mentions one entrepreneur who never works in
the same place two days in a row. Instead, he has several different workspaces and rotates through them to fit the needs
of his Ideal Week.[19]

Vacating isn't the only way to make your workspace work
for you. Another is to optimize your current workspace for
focus. For instance, eliminate items that can easily distract
you and make an effort to beautify your space. When we
designed the Michael Hyatt & Company workspace, we included a quiet room where people can go for deep work, but
we also ensured the entire office was aesthetically pleasing.
No one is required to work in the office, but the entire local
team spends time there every week because it's an optimal
environment for productivity.

Declutter your workspace. Studies show that disorder
does have some benefits, especially for creative work, but
it's terrible for focused execution.[20] According to writer Erin
Doland, researchers at the Princeton Neuroscience Insti-

tute found, "When your environment is cluttered, the chaos restricts your ability to focus. The clutter also limits your brain's ability to process information. Clutter makes you distracted and unable to process information as well as you do in an uncluttered, organized, and serene environment."[21]

If you work in a junky office, it's time to clean it up. I don't care how busy you are; this is a task you should definitely categorize as both urgent and important. Your clutter is getting in your way, whether you realize it or not. I recommend making an appointment with yourself on your calendar to organize your office. If this is far outside your Desire Zone, then maybe you can delegate it to someone else—preferably someone who is really good at organization. This is time (and, if necessary, money) well spent.

Clutter here also refers to your digital workspace. If your computer files are all over the place and there's no rhyme or reason to your folder structure, schedule some time to organize that as well. If you're going to live much of your life on the computer, it should at least be as uncluttered as your office.

Increase your frustration tolerance. If you opt for downhill work too soon and too often, you can improve your focus by improving your frustration tolerance. The longer you can sit with the challenge of important uphill tasks—and the difficult emotions that often come with them—the more effective you'll be and the more likely you'll be to finish your projects and achieve your goals.

The first step is to notice when the impulse to bail comes. If you notice it, you can choose to ignore it. And the more you choose to stick with the uphill task, the stronger your frustration tolerance will become. You're training yourself for focus.[22] But how do you notice? Few things work as well as cultivating mindfulness. The more we are aware of our thinking and emotions, the more likely we are to notice when we're anxious, stressed, or otherwise prone to distraction. According to Fabritius and Hagemann, "Mindfulness training has been found to strengthen the brain's ability to pay attention by increasing your capacity to ignore both internal and external distractions and to focus instead on what's happening in the moment."[23] I find journaling also helps because it allows me to reflect and analyze what worked (or didn't) in my performance.

No Isolator Needed

Taking charge of your day may not only be challenging; it can be terrifying. If all you've ever known is jumping from one fire to another all day, the idea of cutting yourself off from interruptions may leave you to wonder, *Who will put out all those fires if I don't?* I've learned over the years that high-achievers become the go-to problem-solvers for everyone around them. And, as we all know, fixing someone else's problem practically guarantees they'll bring you more problems in the future.

If you want to become free to focus, you can't spend your whole day working on someone else's priorities. That's never going to drive the results you want for yourself. Nor can you let the ease of downhill tasks pull you away from the high-leverage work essential for reaching your goals.

And while we're on that point, take a minute and look at your quarterly goals, your Weekly Big 3, and your Daily Big 3.

What are those worth to you? What would accomplishing them make possible in your life and business? Gernsback's Isolator might be a clever invention, but you don't need one. Now that you're empowered to beat interruptions and distractions, nothing can stand between you and your most important projects and goals.

A PLAN TO MINIMIZE DISRUPTIONS

It's time to use the strategies and practices in this chapter to develop your personalized action plan for minimizing disruptions in your day. Download a copy of the Focus Defense Worksheet at FreeToFocus.com/tools.

Your first goal is to eliminate interruptions. Start by creating an Activation Trigger. Remember, this is just a simple reminder of your intention, a prompt to help you implement positive action. In this case, it could be something like hanging a Do Not Disturb sign on your door. Next, list the obstacles you think could get in the way. Then, predetermine your response—your Anticipation Tactic.

Repeat this same process for distractions. When you're done, you'll have clear, actionable strategy for banishing the time bandits once and for all.

Put Your Focus to Work

Amateurs sit and wait for inspiration, the rest of us
just get up and go to work.

STEPHEN KING

I n 1816 Francis Ronalds looped eight miles of wire between
two poles in his backyard. Sending signals over the wire
keyed to letters of the alphabet, he was able to send messages that could be received and decoded in an instant. Before
Ronalds's invention of the telegraph, messages could only
travel as fast as they could be physically transmitted over the
necessary distance. Ronalds wrote the British Admiralty with
news of his extraordinary breakthrough, expecting an eager
reception. Instead, an official responded and said the government had no need of his invention. As historian Ian Mortimer explains, "The Admiralty believed that the semaphore
system they had then recently adopted—that is, men waving
flags at each other—was superior."[1] Can you believe it!

It's easy to mock the officials, but we're all prone to the same basic mistake. We overvalue our current systems and resist change—even if that change will bring about immediate, life-altering benefits. I tell this story because you're now faced with a choice: you can opt for a new and transformative approach to productivity—or you can wave flags. The old methods of productivity have taken us as far as they can and burned up many of us along the way. It's time for a new approach. The world caught on to Ronalds's invention and set a communications revolution in motion that still affects us today. I want you to join the *Free to Focus* productivity revolution.

We started this book with an unusual call to Stop. I told you then that the best way to start was by stopping, because I was certain you were spending far too much time and energy on things that ultimately didn't matter. But that was a long time ago. That was before you learned how to articulate your *why* for increasing your productivity, before you learned how to cut the unnecessary tasks and time-wasters from your schedule, and before you learned how to put all these principles into action. Now, armed with what we've learned, it's time to *begin*.

Your *Free to Focus* Success Path

Here's a start-to-finish success path you can follow beginning right now.

1. **Clear the decks.** Carve out some margin so you can focus on implementing *Free to Focus*. Triage your calendar and make whatever arrangements you need to

buy yourself some time. If you have an assistant, loop them into this process.

2. **Set your baseline.** Use the *Free to Focus* Productivity Assessment I mentioned at the start of the book to establish your productivity baseline. You can find that at FreeToFocus.com/assessment.

3. **Clarify your objective.** Get clear on the goal of productivity. It's about doing more of the right things, not simply doing more. High performance for its own sake is just burnout waiting to happen.

4. **Find true north.** Use the Task Filter and Freedom Compass to identify what's working for you now and what's not.

5. **Schedule margin.** Reserve mornings, evenings, and weekends for rejuvenation so you've got the mental and emotional energy to maximize your focus.

6. **Prune the overgrowth.** Create a Not-to-Do List using your Freedom Compass and start eliminating everything you can from your calendar and task list—both now and going forward.

7. **Stop thinking about it.** Look at your regular activities—especially morning and evening, workday startup and shutdown—and establish some rituals you can follow. Invent the wheel once and it'll keep rolling even if you stop paying attention. Next, identify three or four necessary tasks or processes you can automate, starting right away.

8. **Offload everything you can.** Using the Delegation Hierarchy, start offloading tasks to other members of your team. Don't have a team? Find some freelance help. The

more time you spend in your Desire Zone the greater the contribution you'll make, and that means you can afford the help.

9. **Plan an Ideal Week.** The future is fuzzy. Give it some firm lines by establishing *when* you want to do *what*. This is the best way to ensure you get the margin you need and have time to focus on what matters most.

10. **Design your week and day.** Use the Weekly Preview along with the Weekly and Daily Big 3 to keep track of your goals and key projects and execute your essential tasks, day in and out.

11. **Beat interruptions and distractions.** Interruptions and distractions can derail your day, but they don't have to. You have far more control over disruptions than you might realize. Follow the suggestions in chapter 9 and banish them for good.

It can take a while to get dialed in, but you've got what it takes. As a high-achiever, you're not only up for a challenge, you're also an expert in rising to the occasion and reaping the rewards.

Staying on Track

Once you start using the *Free to Focus* system, it will help you maintain momentum—even when new obstacles and challenges arise. And they will. High-achievers are always moving. Hold on to your Freedom Compass and let it guide you through the twists and turns. Now you know how to navigate. When faced with roadblocks to your productivity, just go back to the three primary steps of the system: *Stop*, *Cut*, and *Act*. These steps provide a rapid course correction so you can stay on track even in your busiest seasons.

Stop. No one makes smart decisions in a frenzy of activity. Instead, press pause. Step away from your desk. Take a walk outside. Get a good night's sleep—whatever it takes to clear your head. Then evaluate. Reflect on your true objective, get clear on why it matters, and consider any changes you may need to make to your strategy in order to achieve it.

Cut. Odds are you don't just feel as if you have too much to do. You actually have too much to do. Even after you've implemented the *Free to Focus* system, you may find tasks creeping onto your list and slowly encroaching on your productivity. Use what you've learned to eliminate, automate, and delegate as many of these tasks as possible.

Act. Now that you have a clear path, it's time to get moving. Starting is half the battle, so identify next steps that will give you a quick sense of momentum. The other half of the battle is staying focused. Interruptions and distractions can sabotage even your best efforts. Identify the strategies you'll use to stay focused—whether it's switching off your notifications or hanging a Do Not Disturb sign on your office door. You'll be amazed how much you can accomplish when you're free to focus.

Remember what Herbert Simon said at the start: "Information consumes the attention of its recipients." We work in the Distraction Economy. Attention is a scarce resource, and almost everyone out there is trying to capitalize on your focus. If you're not careful, you'll spend your most valuable resource to achieve someone else's goals.

The solution is to leverage your focus and make progress on the initiatives and projects that will drive your success. That's what *Free to Focus* has shown you how to do. Just as important, it's shown you how to finally get your margin back. Working forty (or even fewer) hours a week means ample time to invest in your most important relationships, your health and hobbies, and all the other things that keep you sharp and productive for the long haul.

So start implementing these strategies. Start taking control of your schedule and maximizing your energy for the things that matter. Start a productivity revolution in your business. Start achieving more by doing less.

Acknowledgments

Writing is difficult, arduous work. It requires years (in some cases, decades) of research, practice, feedback, and refinement—especially a practical book like this one that promises readers they can achieve more by doing less. This book would not exist if it were not for the influence of my mentors, colleagues, clients, customers, and family.

Of my mentors, there are many. I benefited from their books, workshops, and personal coaching. These include David Allen, Ken Blanchard, Larry Bossidy, Stephen R. Covey, Charles Duhigg, Carol Dweck, Peter F. Drucker, Todd Duncan, Tim Ferriss, Daniel Harkavy, Charles Hobbs, Gary Keller, Jim Loehr, Leslie H. Matthies, Chris McChesney, Greg McKeown, Dan Meub, Ilene Muething, Cal Newport, Hyrum W. Smith, Dan Sullivan, Rory Vaden, and Stephanie Winston. My work is built on the foundation of yours.

Joel Miller, our chief content officer at Michael Hyatt & Company, drafted this manuscript using the content of my course by the same name, assorted blog posts, podcasts, and webinars, and my interactions with students both online and off. He (and collaborator Allen Harris) worked tirelessly to finish this project in the midst of an unusually busy season in our business. I am grateful for Joel's ability to analyze, synthesize, and organize my content into final form.

My literary agent, Bryan Norman of Alive Communications, is an invaluable part of our team. He is my trusted advisor for all things related to my publishing. Not only is he crazy-smart, but he's also exceedingly responsive and flawless in his execution. His quick wit and light heart are the icing on the cake.

I am grateful to my editor, Chad Allen, for his vision, creative input, and patience in working with Joel and me on this project. His enthusiasm for this project was contagious and provided the creative fuel we needed to carry it across the goal line.

I would also like to thank all my friends at Baker Books, including Dwight Baker, Brian Vos, Mark Rice, Patti Brinks, and Barb Barnes. This is our third project together, and we have several more to come. I am deeply grateful for our publishing partnership. As an author, I could not be happier.

My wife, Gail, is a constant source of encouragement. Nothing ever makes it into print without her input. I test all my ideas on her first. Gratefully, she jumps in with a joyful and supportive heart. She is also not bashful in expressing her opinion—and I am better for it. She constantly challenges me to say things in a way that is more clear, more simple, and more engaging.

It's difficult to achieve maximum productivity without a great executive assistant. In my nearly four-decade career, three stand out as extraordinary. Tricia Sciortino was my first *virtual* executive assistant. By her own example, she demonstrated that executive assistants are capable of way more than I ever thought possible. Not surprisingly, she is now the president of Belay Solutions, now the world's premier provider of virtual assistant services.

Suzie Barbour served as my executive assistant after Tricia. She, too, did an amazing job—so much so that we promoted her to supervise our internal pool of executive assistants. We then promoted her again. She is currently our Director of Operations. She continues to exceed my expectations, raising the bar on what is possible.

Jim Kelly is my current executive assistant. He anticipates my needs, not only before I articulate them, but often before I am even conscious of them. My only explanation is that he is a mind reader. He does all this with unusual professionalism, kindness, and zero drama.

I especially want to thank the alumni of my *Free to Focus* online course and BusinessAccelerator clients, including those who have shared their stories in this book: Rene Banglesdorf, Roy Barberi, Mariel Diaz, Matt Lapp, Caleb Roney, and Stephen Roney. You are more than customers and clients; you are my teachers.

Finally, I would be remiss if I didn't mention my amazing team at Michael Hyatt & Company. They inspire me every day and enable me to do what I do best. They are truly the #bestteamever. These include Adam Hill, Aleshia Curry, Andrew Fockel, Chad Cannon, Charae Price, Courtney Baker, Danielle Rodgers, Dave Yankowiak, Deidra Romero, Jamie

Cartwright, Jamie Hess, Jeremy Lott, Jim Kelly, Joel Miller, John Meese, Justin Barbour, Kyle Wyley, Larry Wilson, Mandi Rivieccio, Megan Hyatt Miller, Megan Greer, Mike "Verbs" Boyer, Mike Burns, Neal Samudre, Sarah McElroy, Susan Caldwell, and Suzie Barbour.

Notes

Stepping into Focus

1. Herbert A. Simon, "Designing Organizations for an Information-Rich World," *Computers, Communication, and the Public Interest*, ed. Martin Greenberger (Baltimore: Johns Hopkins Press, 1971), 40.

2. Oliver Burkeman, "Attentional Commons," *New Philosopher*, August–October 2017.

3. Richard Ovenden, "Virtual Memory: The Race to Save the Information Age," *Financial Times*, May 19, 2016, https://www.ft.com/content/907fe3a6-1ce3-11e6-b286-cddde55ca122.

4. Brian Dumaine, "The Kings of Concentration," *Inc.*, May 2014, https://www.inc.com/magazine/201405/brian-dumaine/how-leaders-focus-with-distractions.html.

5. Rachel Emma Silverman, "Workplace Distractions: Here's Why You Won't Finish This Article," *Wall Street Journal*, December 11, 2012, https://www.wsj.com/articles/SB10001424127887324339204578173252223022388.

6. Silverman, "Workplace Distractions."

7. Brent D. Peterson and Gaylan W. Nielson, *Fake Work* (New York: Simon Spotlight Entertainment, 2009), xx.

8. Susanna Huth, "Employees Waste 759 Hours Each Year Due to Workplace Distractions," *London Telegraph*, June 22, 2015, https://www.telegraph.co.uk/finance/jobs/11691728/Employees-waste-759-hours-each-year-due-to-workplace-distractions.html. Brigid Schulte, "Work Interruptions Can Cost You 6 Hours a Day," *Washington Post*, June 1, 2015, https://www.washingtonpost.com/news/inspired-life/wp/2015/06/01/interruptions-at-work-can-cost-you-up-to-6-hours-a-day-heres-how-to-avoid-them.

9. Jonathan B. Spira, *Overload!* (New York: Wiley, 2011), xiv.

10. Joseph Carroll, "Time Pressures, Stress Common for Americans," Gallup, January 2, 2008, http://news.gallup.com/poll/103456/Time -Pressures-Stress-Common-Americans.aspx.

11. Maurie Backman, "Work-Related Stress: Is Your Job Making You Sick?" *USA Today*, February 10, 2018, https://www.usatoday.com/story /money/careers/2018/02/10/is-your-job-making-you-sick/110121176/.

12. Jennifer J. Deal, "Always On, Never Done?" Center for Creative Leadership, August 2013, https://s3.amazonaws.com/s3.documentcloud .org/documents/1148838/always-on-never-done.pdf.

13. Patricia Reaney, "Love Them or Loathe Them, Emails Are Here to Stay," Reuters, August 26, 2015, https://www.reuters.com/article/usa -work-emails/love-them-or-loathe-them-emails-are-here-to-stay-survey -idUSL1N10Z29D20150826.

14. According to the same survey, nearly 8 percent check work email at kids' school functions, and more than 6 percent do it at weddings. What's more, 4 percent do it when they or their spouse is in labor, and some even do it at funerals! Melanie Hart, "Hail Mail or Fail Mail?" *TechTalk*, June 24, 2015, https://techtalk.gfi.com/hail-mail-or-fail-mail.

15. Lewis Carroll, *Through the Looking Glass* (New York: Macmillan, 1897), 42.

16. Alan Schwarz, "Workers Seeking Productivity in a Pill Are Abusing A.D.H.D. Drugs," *New York Times*, April 18, 2015, https://www .nytimes.com/2015/04/19/us/workers-seeking-productivity-in-a-pill-are -abusing-adhd-drugs.html. Carl Cederström, "Like It or Not, 'Smart Drugs' Are Coming to the Office," *Harvard Business Review*, May 19, 2016, https://hbr.org/2016/05/like-it-or-not-smart-drugs-are-coming-to -the-office. Andrew Leonard, "How LSD Microdosing Became the Hot New Business Trip," *Rolling Stone*, November 20, 2015, https://www.roll ingstone.com/culture/features/how-lsd-microdosing-became-the-hot -new-business-trip-20151120. Lila MacLellan, "The Science behind the 15 Most Common Smart Drugs," *Quartz*, September 20, 2017, https:// qz.com/1064224/the-science-behind-the-15-most-common-smart-drugs/.

17. Burkeman, "Attentional Commons."

Chapter 1 Formulate

1. Quoted in Nikil Saval, *Cubed: A Secret History of the Workplace* (New York: Doubleday, 2014), 50. See the full discussion of Taylor and Taylorism on pages 45–62. Taylor's disciples later applied his approach to office workers, determining how long it took for basic tasks, such as opening desk drawers and turning in a swivel chair. (In case you're

wondering, the times are .04 and .009 minutes, respectively.) "Taylor and his disciples turned efficiency into a science," economist Jeremy Rifkin said. "They inaugurated a new ethos. Efficiency was officially christened the dominant value of the contemporary age." See Rifkin, *Time Wars* (New York: Touchstone, 1989), 131–32.

2. Lydia Saad, "The '40-Hour' Workweek Is Actually Longer—by Seven Hours," Gallup, August 29, 2014, http://news.gallup.com/poll/17 5286/hour-workweek-actually-longer-seven-hours.aspx.

3. Heather Boushey and Bridget Ansel, "Overworked America," Washington Center for Equitable Growth, May 2016, http://cdn.equitable growth.org/wp-content/uploads/2016/05/16164629/051616-overworked -america.pdf.

4. Leslie A. Perlow and Jessica L. Porter, "Making Time Off Predictable—and Required," *Harvard Business Review*, October 2009, https:// hbr.org/2009/10/making-time-off-predictable-and-required.

5. Josef Pieper, *Leisure as the Basis of Culture*, trans. Alexander Dru (San Francisco: Ignatius, 2009), 20.

6. "The North American Workplace Survey," Workplace Trends, June 29, 2015, https://workplacetrends.com/north-american-workplace-survey/.

7. "The Employee Burnout Crisis: Study Reveals Big Workplace Challenge in 2017," Kronos, January 9, 2017, https://www.kronos.com/about -us/newsroom/employee-burnout-crisis-study-reveals-big-workplace -challenge-2017.

8. Willis Towers Watson, "Global Benefits Attitudes Survey 2015/16," https://www.willistowerswatson.com/en/insights/2016/02/global-benefit -attitudes-survey-2015-16.

9. Michael Blanding, "National Health Costs Could Decrease If Managers Reduce Work Stress," Harvard Business School Working Knowledge, January 26, 2015, https://hbswk.hbs.edu/item/national-health-costs -could-decrease-if-managers-reduce-work-stress.

10. Chris Weller, "Japan Is Facing a 'Death by Overwork' Problem," *Business Insider*, October 18, 2017, http://www.businessinsider.com/wh at-is-karoshi-japanese-word-for-death-by-overwork-2017-10. Jake Adelstein, who has worked in Japanese media, said 80-to-100-hour weeks are routine: "Japan Is Literally Working Itself to Death: How Can It Stop?" *Forbes*, October 30, 2017, https://www.forbes.com/sites/adelsteinjake /2017/10/30/japan-is-literally-working-itselfto-death-how-can-it-stop.

11. "Man on Cusp of Having Fun Suddenly Remembers Every Single One of His Responsibilities," *Onion*, May 30, 2013, http://www.the onion.com/article/man-on-cusp-of-having-fun-suddenly-remembers -every-32632.

12. Liz Alderman, "In Sweden, an Experiment Turns Shorter Workdays into Bigger Gains," *New York Times*, May 20, 2016, https://www.ny times.com/2016/05/21/business/international/in-sweden-an-experiment -turns-shorter-workdays-into-bigger-gains.html.
13. "Ford Factory Workers Get 40-Hour Week," History.com, http:// www.history.com/this-day-in-history/ford-factory-workers-get-40-hour -week.
14. "Ford Factory Workers," History.com.
15. Basil the Great, "Letter 2 (to Gregory of Nazianzus)," trans. Roy J. Deferrari (Cambridge: Harvard University Press, 1926), Loeb 190, 1.9.

Chapter 2 Evaluate

1. See the findings summarized in Anders Ericsson and Robert Pool, *Peak* (New York: Houghton Mifflin Harcourt, 2016). Also see Mihaly Csikszentmihalyi, *Flow* (New York: Harper Perennial, 2008).
2. See Tom Rath, *StrengthsFinder 2.0* (New York: Gallup, 2007), 105–8.
3. To go deeper on the subject of limiting beliefs, including a process for transforming them into liberating truths, see "Step 1: Believe the Possibility" in my book, *Your Best Year Ever* (Grand Rapids: Baker Books, 2018), 25–62.

Chapter 3 Rejuvenate

1. Alexandra Michel, "Participation and Self-Entrapment," *The Sociological Quarterly* 55, 2014, http://alexandramichel.com/Self-entrap ment.pdf.
2. John M. Nevison, "Overtime Hours: The Rule of Fifty," New Leaf Management, December 1997.
3. Morten T. Hansen, *Great at Work* (New York: Simon and Schuster, 2018), 46. Based on Hansen's research, workers might profitably work more than fifty hours a week, but he advises against it. Says cognitive psychologist Daniel J. Levitin, "A sixty-hour work week, although 50% longer than a forty-hour work week, reduces productivity by 25%, so it takes two hours of overtime to accomplish one hour of work." *The Organized Mind* (New York: Dutton, 2016), 307.
4. Sarah Green Carmichael, "The Research Is Clear: Long Hours Backfire for People and for Companies," *Harvard Business Review*, August 19, 2015, https://hbr.org/2015/08/the-research-is-clear-long-hours-back fire-for-people-and-for-companies.
5. Bambi Francisco Roizen, "Elon Musk: Work Twice as Hard as Others," Vator.TV, December 23, 2010, http://vator.tv/news/2010-12-23 -elon-musk-work-twice-as-hard-as-others.

6. Michael D. Eisner, *Work in Progress* (New York: Hyperion, 1999), 301.

7. Jeffrey M. Jones, "In U.S., 40% Get Less Than Recommended Amount of Sleep," Gallup, December 19, 2013, http://news.gallup.com/poll/166553/less-recommended-amount-sleep.aspx.

8. Diane S. Lauderdale et al., "Objectively Measured Sleep Characteristics among Early-Middle-Aged Adults," *American Journal of Epidemiology* 164, no.1 (July 1, 2006), https://academic.oup.com/aje/article/164/1/5/81104.

9. Tanya Basu, "CEOs Like PepsiCo's Indra Nooyi Brag They Get 4 Hours of Sleep. That's Toxic," *The Daily Beast*, August 11, 2018, https://www.thedailybeast.com/ceos-like-pepsicos-indra-nooyi-brag-they-get-4-hours-of-sleep-thats-toxic. Katie Pisa, "Why Missing a Night of Sleep Can Damage Your IQ," CNN, April 20, 2015, https://www.cnn.com/2015/04/01/business/sleep-and-leadership. Geoff Colvin, "Do Successful CEOs Sleep Less Than Everyone Else?" *Fortune*, November 18, 2015, http://fortune.com/2015/11/18/sleep-habits-donald-trump. According to one study, 42 percent of leaders get six hours of sleep or less each night. Christopher M. Barnes, "Sleep Well, Lead Better," *Harvard Business Review*, September–October 2018.

10. Nick van Dam and Els van der Helm, "The Organizational Cost of Insufficient Sleep," *McKinsey Quarterly*, February 2016, https://www.mckinsey.com/business-functions/organization/our-insights/the-organizational-cost-of-insufficient-sleep.

11. N.J. Taffinder et al., "Effect of Sleep Deprivation on Surgeons' Dexterity on Laparoscopy Simulator," *The Lancet*, October 10, 1998, http://www.thelancet.com/pdfs/journals/lancet/PIIS0140673698000348.pdf.

12. Maggie Jones, "How Little Sleep Can You Get Away With?" *New York Times Magazine*, April 15, 2011, http://www.nytimes.com/2011/04/17/magazine/mag-17Sleep-t.html.

13. On these and related points, see Shawn Stevenson, *Sleep Smarter* (New York: Rodale, 2016); David K. Randall, *Dreamland* (New York: Norton, 2012); and Penelope A. Lewis, *The Secret World of Sleep* (New York: Palgrave Macmillan, 2014).

14. Lewis, *The Secret World of Sleep*, 18.

15. Jeff Bezos, "Why Getting 8 Hours of Sleep Is Good for Amazon Shareholders," Thrive Global, November 30, 2016, https://www.thriveglobal.com/stories/7624-jeff-bezos-why-getting-8-hours-of-sleep-is-good-for-amazon-shareholders.

16. Matthew J. Belvedere, "Why Aetna's CEO Pays Workers Up to $500 to Sleep," CNBC, April 5, 2016, https://www.cnbc.com/2016/04/05/why-aetnas-ceo-pays-workers-up-to-500-to-sleep.html.

17. Alex Hern, "Netflix's Biggest Competitor? Sleep," *Guardian*, April 18, 2017, https://www.theguardian.com/technology/2017/apr/18/netflix-competitor-sleep-uber-facebook.

18. Alex Soojung-Kim Pang, *Rest* (New York: Basic, 2016), 110–128.

19. Barbara Holland, *Endangered Pleasures* (Boston: Little, Brown, 1995), 38.

20. For optimizing your nighttime sleep, I recommend Shawn Stevenson's *Sleep Smarter* and for naptime Sara C. Mednick's *Take a Nap! Change Your Life* (New York: Workman, 2006).

21. "Just One-in-Five Employees Take Actual Lunch Break," Right Management ThoughtWire, October 16, 2012, https://www.right.com/wps/wcm/connect/right-us-en/home/thoughtwire/categories/media-center/Just+OneinFive+Employees+Take+Actual+Lunch+Break.

22. "We're Not Taking Enough Lunch Breaks. Why That's Bad for Business," NPR, March 5, 2015, https://www.npr.org/sections/thesalt/2015/03/05/390726886/were-not-taking-enough-lunch-breaks-why-thats-bad-for-business.

23. "Physical Activity and Health," Centers for Disease Control and Prevention, February 13, 2018, https://www.cdc.gov/physicalactivity/basics/pa-health/index.htm.

24. "Physical Activity and Health," CDC.

25. Ben Opipari, "Need a Brain Boost? Exercise," *Washington Post*, May 27, 2014, https://www.washingtonpost.com/lifestyle/wellness/need-a-brain-boost-exercise/2014/05/27/551773f4-db92-11e3-8009-71de85b9c527_story.html.

26. Russell Clayton, "How Regular Exercise Helps You Balance Work and Family," *Harvard Business Review*, January 3, 2014, https://hbr.org/2014/01/how-regular-exercise-helps-you-balance-work-and-family.

27. Clayton, "Regular Exercise."

28. Tom Jacobs, "Want to Get Rich? Get Fit," *Pacific Standard*, January 31, 2014, https://psmag.com/social-justice/want-get-rich-get-fit-72515.

29. Henry Cloud, *The Power of the Other* (New York: Harper Business, 2016), 9, 81.

30. Emily Stone, "Sitting Near a High-Performer Can Make You Better at Your Job," *KelloggInsight*, May 8, 2017, https://insight.kellogg.northwestern.edu/article/sitting-near-a-high-performer-can-make-you-better-at-your-job.

31. Cloud, *Power of the Other*, 81.

32. Stone, "Sitting Near a High-Performer Can Make You Better at Your Job."

33. Virginia Postrel, *The Future and Its Enemies* (New York: Free Press, 1998), 188.

34. Stuart Brown, *Play* (New York: Avery, 2010), 127.

35. Jeremy Lott, "Hobbies of Highly Effective People," MichaelHyatt .com, November 7, 2017, https://michaelhyatt.com/hobbies-and-effective ness/.

36. Paul Johnson, *Churchill* (New York: Penguin, 2009), 128, 163.

37. Winston S. Churchill, *Painting as a Pastime* (London: Unicorn, n.d.). He wrote this essay in 1948.

38. Shirley S. Wang, "Coffee Break? Walk in the Park? Why Unwinding Is Hard," *Wall Street Journal*, August 30, 2011, https://www.wsj.com /articles/SB10001424053111904199404576538260326965724.

39. Chris Mooney, "Just Looking at Nature Can Help Your Brain Work Better, Study Finds," *Washington Post*, May 26, 2015, https://www .washingtonpost.com/news/energy-environment/wp/2015/05/26/viewing -nature-can-help-your-brain-work-better-study-finds/.

40. Ruth Ann Atchley et al., "Creativity in the Wild: Improving Creative Reasoning through Immersion in Natural Settings," *PLOS One* 7, no. 12 (December 12, 2012), http://journals.plos.org/plosone/article?id =10.1371/journal.pone.0051474.

41. Netta Weinstein, Andrew K. Przybylski, and Richard M. Ryan, "Can Nature Make Us More Caring?" *Personality and Social Psychology Bulletin*, August 5, 2009, https://journals.sagepub.com/doi/abs/10.1177 /0146167209341649. Diane Mapes, "Looking at Nature Makes You Nicer," NBCNews.com, October 14, 2009, http://www.nbcnews.com/id/33243959 /ns/health-behavior/t/looking-nature-makes-you-nicer.

42. Jill Suttie, "How Nature Can Make You Kinder, Happier, and More Creative," *Greater Good*, March 2, 2016, https://greatergood.berkeley .edu/article/item/how_nature_makes_you_kinder_happier_more_crea tive. Cecily Maller et al., "Healthy Nature Healthy People: 'Contact with Nature' as an Upstream Health Promotion Intervention for Populations," *Health Promotion International* 21, no. 1 (March 2006), https://academic .oup.com/heapro/article/21/1/45/646436. "How Does Nature Impact Our Wellbeing?" *Taking Charge of Your Health & Wellbeing* (University of Minnesota), https://www.takingcharge.csh.umn.edu/enhance-your -wellbeing/environment/nature-and-us/how-does-nature-impact-our- wellbeing.

43. "Unplugged for 24 hours," *New Philosopher*, February–April 2016.

Chapter 4 Eliminate

1. Steve Turner, *Beatles '66* (New York: Ecco, 2016), 47.

2. As Friederike Fabritius and Hans W. Hagemann put it, "No one questions the fact that you are unavailable when you're already in an

important meeting, but there's often an unspoken assumption that when you aren't in a meeting, you're free. And yet when you need to focus, you are in an important meeting—with *yourself.*" *The Leading Brain* (New York: TarcherPerigree, 2017), 91–92.

3. William Ury, *The Power of a Positive No* (New York: Bantam, 2007), 10–15.

4. Ury, *Positive No*, 14.

5. Ury, *Positive No*, 16–18.

Chapter 5 Automate

1. "Ritual," Dictionary.com, http://www.dictionary.com/browse/ritual.

2. Mason Currey, *Daily Rituals* (New York: Knopf, 2015), xiv. Also see Pang's discussion of morning routines in *Rest*, 75–92.

3. Atul Gawande, "The Checklist," *New Yorker*, December 10, 2007, https://www.newyorker.com/magazine/2007/12/10/the-checklist. See also Gawande's book, *The Checklist Manifesto* (New York: Metropolitan Books, 2009).

Chapter 6 Delegate

1. Ashley V. Whillans et al., "Buying Time Promotes Happiness," *PNAS*, August 8, 2017, http://www.pnas.org/content/114/32/8523.

2. Adapted and expanded from Stephanie Winston, *The Organized Executive* (New York: Norton, 1983), 249–50.

Chapter 7 Consolidate

1. John Naish, "Is Multi-tasking Bad for Your Brain? Experts Reveal the Hidden Perils of Juggling Too Many Jobs," *Daily Mail*, August 11, 2009, http://www.dailymail.co.uk/health/article-1205669/Is-multi-tasking-bad-brain-Experts-reveal-hidden-perils-juggling-jobs.html.

2. Cal Newport, *Deep Work* (New York: Grand Central, 2014), 42.

3. Christine Rosen, "The Myth of Multitasking," *New Atlantis*, no. 20, Spring 2008, https://www.thenewatlantis.com/publications/the-myth-of-multitasking.

4. Rosen, "Myth of Multitasking."

5. Today we usually produce our *Lead to Win* podcast three to four episodes at a time. We set aside one day a month for recording.

6. Jason Fried and David Heinemeier, *ReWork* (New York: Crown Business, 2010), 105.

7. Silverman, "Workplace Distractions."

8. William Shakespeare, *As You Like It* 2.7.139–42.

9. Garson O'Toole has the backstory on the line here: "Plans Are Worthless, But Planning Is Everything," *Quote Investigator*, November 18, 2017, https://quoteinvestigator.com/2017/11/18/planning.

10. I first encountered the idea behind the Ideal Week in Todd Duncan's work, especially *Time Traps* (Nashville: Thomas Nelson, 2006), and Stephanie Winston's *The Organized Executive* (New York: Warner Books, 1994). I've adapted the idea over the years as I've applied it to my own practice, as well as helping my coaching clients.

11. Pang, *Rest*, 53–74.

12. Daniel H. Pink, *When* (New York: Riverhead, 2018), 9–35, 71. Pang echoes this advice in *Rest*; see his discussion on rhythms, 81–85.

13. Rosen, "Myth of Multitasking."

Chapter 8 Designate

1. Air Traffic Organization, *Air Traffic by the Numbers*, Federal Aviation Administration, October 2017, https://www.faa.gov/air_traffic/by _the_numbers/media/Air_Traffic_by_the_Numbers_2017_Final.pdf.

2. Kiera Butler et al., "Harrowing, Heartbreaking Tales of Overworked Americans," *Mother Jones*, July/August 2011, https://www.mother jones.com/politics/2011/06/stories-overworked-americans.

3. Matt Potter, "Harrowing Tales of Lindbergh Field Air Traffic," *San Diego Reader*, December 6, 2013, https://www.sandiegoreader.com/news /2013/dec/06/ticker-harrowing-tales-lindbergh-field-landings.

4. J. D. Meier presents a similar concept in his book, *Getting Results the Agile Way* (Bellevue: Innovative Playhouse, 2010), 56, 88.

5. See Stephen R. Covey, *The 7 Habits of Highly Effective People* (New York: Simon and Schuster, 2004), 160ff; Stephen R. Covey, A. Roger Merrill, and Rebecca R. Merrill, *First Things First* (New York: Fireside, 1994), 37ff. The simple four-sector grid was developed by Covey, based on an observation of Gen. Eisenhower, quoting an anonymous college president: "'I have two kinds of problems, the urgent and the important. The urgent are not important, and the important are never urgent.' Now this, I think, represents a dilemma of modern man." Dwight D. Eisenhower, "Address at the Second Assembly of the World Council of Churches," Evanston, Illinois, August 19, 1954, https://www.presidency .ucsb.edu/documents/address-the-second-assembly-the-world-council -churches-evanston-illinois.

6. Meier presents a version of this idea in *Getting Results the Agile Way*, 56, 65. He calls it the Rule of 3 and says that picking three items to focus on works because our minds naturally organize in threes. See Chris Bailey, *The Productivity Project* (New York: Crown Business, 2016), 40.

7. Gwen Moran, "What Successful Leaders' To-Do Lists Look Like," *Fast Company*, March 25, 2014, https://www.fastcompany.com/3028094 /what-successful-leaders-to-do-lists-look-like.

8. Christina DesMarais, "The Daily Habits of 35 People at the Top of Their Game," *Inc.*, July 13, 2015, https://www.inc.com/christina -desmarais/the-daily-habits-of-35-people-at-the-top-of-their-game.html.

9. Seneca, *On the Shortness of Life*, trans. C.D.N. Costa (New York: Penguin, 2005), 1, 2, 4.

Chapter 9 Activate

1. Matt Novak, "Thinking Cap," *Pacific Standard*, May 2, 2013, https://psmag.com/environment/thinking-cap-gernsback-isolator-56505.

2. Nikil Saval covers the history of this trend in his book *Cubed*, and Cal Newport counts the cost it levies on focus in *Deep Work*.

3. "Can We Chat? Instant Messaging Apps Invade the Workplace," *ReportLinker*, June 8, 2017, https://www.reportlinker.com/insight/instant -messaging-apps-invade-workplace.html.

4. I first started thinking about the distinctions between instant and de-layed communication in 2017 when noticing the negative effect of instant communication on my own team. See Allan Christensen, "How Doist Makes Remote Work Happen," ToDoist Blog, May 25, 2017, https://blog .todoist.com/2017/05/25/how-doist-works-remote; Amir Salihefendic, "Why We're Betting Against Real-Time Team Messaging," Doist, June 13, 2017, https://blog.doist.com/why-were-betting-against-real-time-team -messaging-521804a3da09; and Aleksandra Smelianska, "Asynchronous Communication for Remote Teams," YouTeam.io, https://youteam.io/ blog/asynchronous-communication-for-remote-teams.

5. David Pierce, "Turn Off Your Push Notifications. All of Them," *Wired*, July 23, 2017, https://www.wired.com/story/turn-off-your-push -notifications/.

6. "'Infomania' Worse Than Marijuana," BBC News, April 22, 2005, http://news.bbc.co.uk/2/hi/uk_news/4471607.stm.

7. Fabritius and Hagemann, *Leading Brain*, 83.

8. Burkeman, "Attentional Commons."

9. Novak, "Thinking Cap."

10. Naish, "Is Multi-tasking Bad for Your Brain?"

11. Clay Shirky, "Why I Just Asked My Students to Put Their Laptops Away," Medium, September 8, 2014, https://medium.com/@cshirky/why -i-just-asked-my-students-to-put-their-laptops-away-7f5f7c50f368.

12. Aaron Gouveia, "Everything You've Always Wanted to Know about Wasting Time in the Office," SFGate.com, July 28, 2013, https://www

.sfgate.com/jobs/salary/article/2013-Wasting-Time-at-Work-Survey
-4374026.php.

13. Adam Gazzaley and Larry Rosen, *The Distracted Mind* (Cambridge: MIT Press, 2016), 165–66.

14. See David Rock, *Your Brain at Work* (New York: HarperBusiness, 2009), 55.

15. Edward M. Hallowell, *Driven to Distraction at Work* (Boston: Harvard Business Review Press, 2015), 6.

16. Chris Bailey, *HyperFocus* (New York: Viking, 2018), 105–6; Benjamin Hardy, *Willpower Doesn't Work* (New York: Hachette, 2018), 192; and Simone M. Ritter and Sam Ferguson, "Happy Creativity: Listening to Happy Music Facilitates Divergent Thinking," *PLOS One*, September 6, 2017, https://journals.plos.org/plosone/article?id=10.1371/journal .pone.0182210.

17. Dean Burnett, "Does Music Really Help You Concentrate?" *The Guardian*, August 20, 2016, https://www.theguardian.com/education /2016/aug/20/does-music-really-help-you-concentrate.

18. See Fabritius and Hagemann, *Leading Brain*, 21–22, 28, 191.

19. Hardy, *Willpower Doesn't Work*, 190–95.

20. On the pluses see Tim Harford, *Messy: The Power of Disorder to Transform our Lives* (New York: Riverhead, 2016).

21. Erin Doland, "Scientists Find Physical Clutter Negatively Affects Your Ability to Focus, Process Information," Unclutterer.com, March 29, 2011, https://unclutterer.com/2011/03/29/scientists-find-physical-clutter -negatively-affects-your-ability-to-focus-process-information/.

22. See the chapter on distractions in Rock, *Your Brain at Work*, 45–59.

23. Fabritius and Hagemann, *Leading Brain*, 102.

Put Your Focus to Work

1. Ian Mortimer, *Millennium* (New York: Pegasus, 2016), 237–38.

Index

Michael Hyatt is the founder and CEO of Michael Hyatt & Company, a leadership coaching and development firm twice listed on the *Inc. 5000* list of fastest-growing US companies. A longtime publishing executive, Michael is the former chairman and CEO of Thomas Nelson, now part of HarperCollins. He is a *New York Times*, *Wall Street Journal*, and *USA Today* bestselling author of several books, including *Your Best Year Ever*, *Living Forward*, and *Platform: Get Noticed in a Noisy World*. Michael is the creator of the *Full Focus Planner*, which combines quarterly goal-tracking and daily productivity in a proven system for personal and professional achievement. His blog and weekly podcast, *Lead to Win*, are go-to resources for hundreds of thousands of entrepreneurs, executives, and aspiring leaders. Michael and his wife of forty years, Gail, have five daughters, three sons-in-law, and eight grandchildren. They live just outside Nashville, Tennessee. Learn more at **MichaelHyatt.com**.

What's Stopping You from Accomplishing Your Biggest Priorities?

Receive instant clarity on how you can improve your productivity with Michael Hyatt's Productivity Assessment™.

- Measure your productivity against ten key metrics and identify what you're doing well—and what needs improvement.

- Gain powerful insight into where your productivity is right now so you can take the steps to make it better.

- Discover your productivity score for maximum clarity.

Take the free assessment at

FreeToFocus.com/assessment

FULL

F⊘CUS

PLANNER

Plan Your Year, Design Your Days, and Achieve Your Biggest Goals.

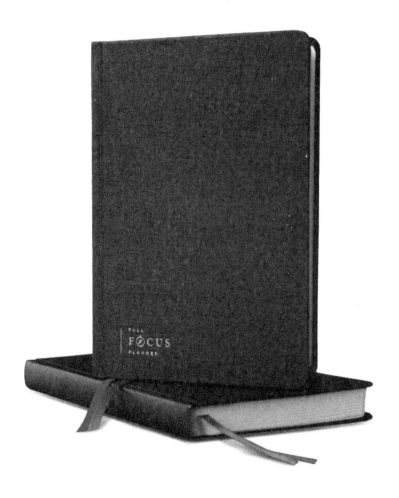

M ichael Hyatt's bestselling paper planner serves as the perfect intersection between annual goal-setting and daily productivity, helping you achieve what matters most.

The Full Focus Planner includes . . .

Daily Pages: Organize your day with the Daily Big 3 planning framework and task list so you structure your day to focus on your priorities.

Weekly Preview: Get a glimpse of the week ahead so you can achieve clarity and confidence over what your priorities should be for the upcoming week.

Annual Goals: Set powerful goals with the goal detail pages so you can start the process for achieving them.

And More . . .

Claim your Full Focus Planner today at

BUSINESS
ACCELERATOR

SCALE YOUR
BUSINESS
— AND —
ACCELERATE
YOUR RESULTS

BusinessAccelerator is Michael Hyatt's executive group
coaching program for business owners and executives who
want to scale their business fast.

In the first year of the program, the average client
experiences . . .

67%	11	35%
GROWTH IN REVENUE	**RECLAIMED HOURS PER WEEK**	**IMPROVEMENT IN WORK-LIFE BALANCE**

64%	66%
INCREASE IN CONFIDENCE	**MORE VACATION TIME**

*Your results will vary, depending on numerous factors, including your implementation of the
program's principles and strategies.*

Find out more at **businessaccelerator.com**